Wicked Smart Golf

Play Better Golf and Shoot Lower Scores *Without* Changing Your Swing

By Michael Leonard

Copyright © 2022 Michael Leonard, All Rights Reserved

The publisher and the author are providing this book and its contents on an "as is" basis and make no representations or warranties of any kind with respect to this book or its contents. The publisher and the author disclaim all such representations and warranties, including but not limited to warranties of healthcare for a particular purpose. In addition, the publisher and the author assume no responsibility for errors, inaccuracies, omissions, or any other inconsistencies herein.

The content of this book is for informational purposes only and is not intended to diagnose, treat, cure, or prevent any condition or disease. You understand that this book is not intended as a substitute for consultation with a licensed practitioner. Please consult with your own physician or healthcare specialist regarding the suggestions and recommendations made in this book. The use of this book implies your acceptance of this disclaimer.

Dedication	10
About the Author	11
Introduction	13
Section I: Mental Game Mastery	18
1. Cultivate an Attitude of Gratitude	21
2. Focus on What You Want	24
3. Reframe Nerves to Minimize First Tee Jitters	27
4. Write on Your Glove	30
5. Keep Breathing	31
6. Change Your Body Language	32
7. Watch Your Self-Talk	34
8. Try Out Neutral Thinking	37
9. Master Your Mind with Meditation	39
10. Visualize Success	41
Off-Course Visualization	42
On-Course Visualization	42
11. Manage Emotions	44
12. Be Your Own Biggest Fan	45
13. Stay Present	46
14. Create a Memory Bank of Good Shots	47
15. Never Give Up	50
Bonus Video	52
Section II: Practice Like a Pro	53
Not Practicing Enough	55
Not Using an Alignment Aid or Picking a Target	55

Thinking a Jumbo Bucket Will Solve Everything	56
Hitting Too Many Irons	57
Never Playing Practice Holes	57
Ignoring Your Pre-Shot Routine	58
Skipping Short Game and Putting	59
16. Practice with a Plan	61
30-Minute Practice Plan	62
60-Minute Practice Plan	62
17. Never Judge Your Practice Session on Time	64
18. Develop a Tour Tempo	65
19. Record Your Swing (the Right Way)	67
Angle #1: Down the Line	68
Angle #2: Face On	68
20. Change Your Range (Practice inside 125 Yards)	70
21. Set Up for Success	72
22. Perfect Your Pre-Shot Routine on the Range	75
23. Use the 80/20 Practice Rule	78
24. Get Better with Technical Practice	79
25. Use Tiger's 9-Shot Practice Drill	81
26. Mix It Up (Random Practice)	82
27. Two Types of Speed Sessions	83
SuperSpeed Sticks	83
Speed Sessions	83
28. Get Back to Basics	85
29. Dial in Your Distances	86

30. Play a Round on the Range	87
31. Practice Where You Play	88
32. Tee It Forward to Go Low	90
33. Improve Your Physical Conditioning	91
34. Practice Less to Get Better	93
Bonus Video	94
Section III: Peaceful Putting	95
35. Play the Right Putter	99
36. Become "Automatic" on the Greens	101
37. Prepare Your Mind for the Putt	104
38. Simplify Green Reading	105
39. Line Up Putts	107
40. Keep Your Head Down	108
41. Get the Ball to the Hole	109
42. Practice Short Putts Frequently	111
43. Putt Whenever Possible	112
44. Putt with a Fairway Wood or Hybrid	113
45. Invest in an Indoor Putting Green	114
46. Quit Trying to Lag it Close	115
47. Record Your Putting Stroke	116
48. The Best Training Aid for Putting	117
49. How to Give Yourself a Putting Lesson	118
Bonus Video	119
Section IV: Becoming a Wedge Wizard	120
50. Carry the Right Wedges	122
51. Use Bounce to make Better Contact	124

52. Weight Forward with Wedges	126
53. Always Accelerate	127
54. Dial in Two Distances for Each Wedge	128
55. Locate Your Landing Zone	131
56. Forget the Flop	133
57. Quit Fearing the Sand	134
58. Make Practice Difficult	137
59. The Science of Spin	138
60. The Dreaded 40–60-Yard Shots	140
Bonus Video	141
Section V: Playing Wicked Smart Golf	142
61. Get The Right Gear	145
Buy a Rangefinder with Slope	145
Play the Right Clubs	145
Have More Hybrids and Forgiving Clubs	146
Swing the Right Shafts	147
Get the Right Grips	147
62. Get a Game Plan	148
63. Warm Up to Win the Round	149
64. Always Analyze the Shot	151
65. Stay Loyal to Your Pre-Shot Routine	153
66. Only Think About Your Target	155
67. Quit Caring About Your First Shot of the Day	157
68. Never Trust Tee Markers	159
69. Club Up On Approach Shots	160

70. Pre-Set to Play With Confidence	162
71. Minimize Mechanical Swing Thoughts	164
72. Understand How to Play Uneven Lies	166
73. Playing Par 3s	169
74. Playing Par 4s	170
75. Playing Par 5s	171
76. Middle of the Green Magic	172
77. Ditch 3 Wood Off the Deck	174
78. Play Conservatively When Your Swing Is Off	175
79. Never Penalize a Perfect Shot	177
80. Avoid the Dreaded Double Bogey	178
81. Give Up on Guiding Shots	179
82. Respect the Rough	180
Determine the Lie	180
Open the Club Face	181
Avoid Hitting Fairway Woods	181
83. Tee Away from Trouble	183
84. Forget about the Flagstick	184
85. Mash the Mud	186
86. Laser in on Lay Up Shots	187
87. Whipping it in Windy Conditions	189
Rule #1. Study the Wind	189
Rule #2. Choose the Right Club	189
Rule #3. Stay Patient and Commit	190
88. Simplify Your Shots	191

89. Choke Up For Confidence and Control	192
90. Manage Your Misses	193
91. Start Laughing and Learning	194
92. Recap Your Round	195
93. The Two Forms of Focus	197
94. Commit for Certainty	199
95. Accept the Result	200
Bonus Video	200
Section VI: Crushing Your Competition	201
96. Practice Like You Play	204
Competitive Practice	204
97. Avoid Technical Swing Changes Before Tournaments	206
98. Tee It Up with Better Players	208
99. Perfect Your Practice Rounds	210
100. Always Arrive Early	212
101. Reset Your Expectations	213
102. Patience and Persistence Are Key	214
103. Maintain a Mantra	215
104. Master Match Play	216
105. Anticipate Adrenaline	218
106. Quit Worrying About Others	219
107. Nail Your Nutrition	221
108. Exit Your Comfort Zone	222
109. Analyze Your Performance after the Round	223
110. Continue Playing Competitive Events	224
111. Fight until the Finish	225

Becoming a Wicked Smart Golfer	226
Bonuses	228

Dedication

To my parents, Linda and Lonnie, for taking me to the golf course every day for years until I could finally drive myself; for all the golf equipment, lessons, and never-ending encouragement to keep pursuing my dreams.

To my aunt, Bev, uncle Rick (my first golf coach), Gaby, and grandparents, who helped me start playing golf and fueled my passion since I was 10. Thanks for introducing me to the greatest game ever played.

To my high school golf coach, Steve York, who saw my potential and gave me a chance freshman year of high school. He saw my work ethic and potential before I ever did, and I'm eternally grateful as golf has played such a significant role in my life.

To my amazing girlfriend Lori, who never doubted me when I quit my corporate sales job to pursue professional golf and entrepreneurship; for always supporting my golf quest and being my ride or die since I popped the collar on my polo in high school.

Without you all believing in me, this book wouldn't be possible, and my life wouldn't be the same without golf.

Also, a shout-out to all the people who told me I had a bad swing, didn't hit it far enough, was too short, and would never make it in golf. Thanks for pouring gas on my already lit fire and helping me reach my potential. There is no doubt it helped me persevere and become the man and golfer I am today.

About the Author

Hey, fellow golfer, my name is Michael Leonard. I'm a full-time golf writer and the creator of Wicked Smart Golf. Since quitting my corporate career in 2017 to pursue entrepreneurship and professional golf, I've written over 1,000,000 words about the sport and been playing golf for over 20 years.

In high school, I dropped 50 shots in four years (124-74), played college golf in Southern California, and now play competitively in Arizona through the USGA, Arizona Golf Association, and Outlaw Tour. I love testing my game so much that I even went to Q-school in 2019 as an amateur golfer.

So, why did I write this book?

Because I want to help you shoot lower scores *without* changing your swing.

If you're like most golfers, you want to shoot lower scores and will do whatever it takes to get there—whether it's buying new clubs, getting lessons, or hitting an endless amount of golf balls on the driving range.

But after going all-in on my golf dreams since 2017, I've realized that most golfers don't reach their potential for one reason - **they think they need a perfect swing to lower their handicap.**

While improving your swing to become a better ball striker always helps, it's not the most important thing to shoot low scores, especially if you're a recreational golfer or someone without grand aspirations of becoming a professional golfer.

Here's the problem, though… Most advice is hurting your game, NOT helping you shoot lower scores. There's too much information out there and it's easy to get overwhelmed, confused, and frustrated trying to understand the complexity of the golf swing.

My goal is simple—help golfers shoot lower scores and drop their handicap *without* all the technical swing changes. Because let's face it, no matter how good you get, your swing will never be perfect and will always be a work in progress.

Fortunately, you don't need a "perfect" swing to break 100, 90, 80 or become a scratch golfer. And in this book, you will learn 111 easy-to-implement strategies that will lead to shooting lower scores *without* changing your swing.

Introduction

Golf is the most rewarding and most infuriating sport ever. If you've ever picked up a club, you probably know exactly what I mean. A good round of golf and everything is right in the world. A bad round of golf and you question why you spend your time and hard-earned money battling your swing.

Despite the roller coaster of emotions, I love golf and have been chasing the little white ball around since 1997. Without golf, I honestly don't know where I would be in life today.

Golf has been a staple in my life because I think there are so many parallels between the sport and real life. You can never conquer golf and life; instead, it's just a quest to see how much you can learn, improve, and adapt with experience.

This is why a lot of top athletes from every sport play golf—the challenge is intoxicating and addicting. Aside from requiring so much mentally and physically from your body, what makes it so great is the journey never ends. No matter how skilled you become, it's impossible to ever reach the top of the mountain.

Even if you do reach new heights of greatness in the golf world, staying there is impossible. Tiger Woods gave us the best preview in his 2000–2001 season, but, as we all know, it didn't last forever. While the Golf Gods reward hard work, no one can conquer this sport forever. That's what makes the game so much fun.

Ironically, most golfers think we can find and sustain greatness. The optimism inside us all that hopes tomorrow will be a better day and that tomorrow will bring a better swing, better mental game, and lower scores.

While optimism is needed, the key to reaching your potential isn't trying to create the perfect swing. Even with a great swing, you will hit more okay or bad shots than you will perfect shots in any round (even PGA Tour players). But fortunately, even if you hit bad shots in a given round, you can still score lower than you thought possible.

This book will help you with—getting the most out of your game *without* changing your swing. Because if you're the type of player reading this book, you know you have the potential for more and know that better golf is within your reach. As self-help author Jack Canfield said, *"You are not given a dream unless you have the capacity to fulfill it."*

Having a dream or goal to improve and play better golf is step one - the vision to shoot lower scores is 100% necessary. But chances are, you have that already, so now it's up to you to learn, think, and act differently in your practice routines and on the course to get to the next level; whatever your goal, whether it's breaking 90, 80, or becoming a single-digit handicap.

I'm confident this book will help get you there. This is NOT a book about technical and mechanical swing thoughts. There are hundreds of books and endless YouTube videos about those topics, and I'll leave those teaching to individuals much more qualified.

Instead, this is a book you can read quickly, apply to your game, and instantly improve your scores. A book you can always flip open for inspiration but also practical advice. This is the stuff that most people need but information that isn't necessarily available in an organized way. That's why I knew I had to share with the world - I want more people to play better golf and enjoy the challenge this great game brings.

Like most golfers, you probably read the title and thought, *What is this guy talking about? You must change your swing to play better golf.*

Here's the thing; I don't disagree, changing your swing *can* help you shoot lower scores. And swing changes are almost necessary to become a scratch golfer and compete in tournaments. My swing has evolved so much over my 20+ years of playing golf and is continuing to do so to this day; it is night and day different from what it was when I was in high school, college, or even a few years ago.

But that's the point; your golf swing is *always* changing and fine-tuning never stops, even for the best, most accomplished players in the world. As Tiger Woods said, *"Golf is fluid. It's always changing. It's always evolving. First of all, you never master it."*

The golf swing is such a complex move that it's always changing, even for the best players in the world. For example, even Tiger has changed his swing multiple times in his career and he's arguably the greatest player of all time (side note, he's the GOAT in my book, records aside).

Since there are so many moving parts to the golf swing, it's a constant evolution and requires endless tinkering. One day your swing is on fire and the next day, it feels like you couldn't make a good swing if your life depended on it.

A seemingly perfect golf swing doesn't guarantee amazing results every single time, either.

Otherwise, guys like Rory McIlroy, Adam Scott, Tiger Woods, and others would win every tournament. But they don't, despite having amazing swings. The winner each week is the player who can get the ball in the fewest strokes—not the one who has the most sound swing.

While a solid, repeatable swing plays a role in elite golf, all the other skills they have mastered make the real difference. Those are all the skills you can use in your game and will learn about in the upcoming chapters.

There is so much more to playing great golf than having a perfect swing.

I know guys with an incredible swing who can barely break 80 consistently. I also know players with mediocre swings who can break 80 (or par) because of a great short game, solid putting, and incredible course management skills.

Up until a few years ago, I never considered myself a very good ball striker. I don't think a lot of guys I played with would argue otherwise either.

My grip was too weak, my backswing was too slow, and I took it way too far inside on the takeaway. Like most everyday golfers, this often leads to an over-the-top, steep move on the downswing. If my timing wasn't perfect, I would hit a pull, over-the-top cut and frequently hit it thin because of a poor weight transfer in the downswing.

If I'm being honest, my shots were ugly many times. Yet even though I had a less than perfect swing, I seemed to always find a way to break 80 and often a lot better.

Here is a perfect example...

I remember a round in high school when I hit only two greens in regulation. Yes, you read that right; I had only two legitimate looks at birdie on the green. But on that day, I still shot a two-over, 74. That's the power of a great short game, an optimistic attitude and playing strategic golf even if your swing is off that day.

Because honestly, most days, your swing won't be 100%. I've never played a round where I hit every shot 100% perfect and I'm not sure anyone else has either. When Jim Furyk shot the first 58 in a PGA Tour event, even he had missed opportunities.

That's just golf.

Most of your shots are misses—some are good misses while others are bad misses. It's about swinging the swing you have that day and making the most of it.

This book will help you with just that; figuring out how to get the most out of your game every day, regardless of if you have a perfect swing (or if it stays at home while you're at the course).

When you're done reading, I am wildly confident you can shoot 5–10 strokes better *without* any swing changes. While it might not happen overnight, it will happen a lot faster than making tedious swing changes; that I can promise.

Again, you can and should still work on your swing; you probably will keep fine-tuning it until the day you hang up your clubs. But even as you develop your swing more consistently, you can still play great golf with all the skills you are about to learn.

Remember, these tips and tricks only work if you do the work. So don't expect to read this book once, not apply any of the principles, and wonder why your scores aren't dropping.

Like anything in life, you must do the work for it to pay off. As Pele said, *"Success is no accident. It is hard work, perseverance, learning, studying, sacrifice, and most of all, love of what you are doing or learning to do."* But if you're committed, hungry to improve, and ready to tap into your full potential, this golf book is for you.

The key is learning what I have termed - **Wicked Smart Golf**. We'll cover these principles inside the book:

- Section I: Mental Game Mastery
- Section II: Practicing Like a Pro
- Section III: Peaceful Putting
- Section IV: Becoming a Wedge Wizard
- Section V: Playing Wicked Smart Golf
- Section VI: Crushing Your Competition

Each section will build on each other to establish a great foundation to think smarter in practice and on the course. All 111 tips and lessons are short by design - golf is complicated enough, and I don't want to make it any harder. By the time you get to section six, you will have the knowledge to even take your game into competitive events.

Also, this book is much more than just the pages you're about to read, as there are tons of free bonuses for investing in Wicked Smart Golf. At the end of each chapter, visit the bonus section for the accompanying videos. In these section recaps, I'll break down a few points in depth, provide additional resources, and tools to become a Wicked Smart Golfer.

Now, let's get into shooting lower scores *without* changing your swing.

Section I: Mental Game Mastery

Understand how to master your mind for lower scores and more fun every single round

To play better, more consistent golf, practicing your swing or short game more often *isn't* always the answer. You can bomb drivers off the tee, flush irons, and have great touch around the green but still not score as low as you want.

So, why aren't you shooting the type of scores you want despite endless practice?

Your mental game.

As I'm sure you know, golf is as much of a mental challenge as physical. You are not only playing against the golf course and your competitors but also your own mind. It's an internal battle that everyone faces, but some players have the tools to master it, while others fall victim to it.

This is why the best athletes in the world are attracted to golf; they love the mental challenges it presents. Paired with the physical act of trying to groove a consistent swing, it's why Michael Jordan, Tom Brady, Wayne Gretzky, and other all-time athletes play golf.

The truth is golf is almost entirely mental. Yet, when's the last time you practiced your mental game? Or, read a book about how the mind works and how it can help you reach your potential or hold you back in sports?

If you've never worked on the mental side of things, don't beat yourself up... most players haven't either. This is why so many golfers *never* reach their potential; they don't understand how to quiet the mind to play more consistently and use it to their advantage.

Still not convinced the mental game is really that important in golf? Then just look at what some of the best players in the world said about the mental side of the game.

- *"Success in golf depends less on strength of body than upon strength of mind."* - Arnold Palmer
- *"The mind is your greatest weapon. It's the greatest club in your bag. It's also your Achilles' heel."* - Steve Elkington
- *"I am about five inches from being an outstanding golfer. That's the distance my left ear is from my right."* - Ben Crenshaw
- *"Golf is a game that's played on a five-inch course - the distance between your ears."* - Bobby Jones

- *"The game of golf is 90% mental and 10% physical."* - Jack Nicklaus

So, why is golf so challenging and taxing on the mind compared to other sports and activities? Here are my thoughts...

- **Golf requires four to six hours of intense focus.** All it takes is one mental mistake to lose your momentum and turn a good round into a bad one quickly. It's why sometimes, after long days, you're not only physically tired but mentally exhausted. A round of golf requires you to battle inner demons, calculate distances on every shot, and keep your mind in the right place to play your best golf.
- **You must battle the course, the conditions, your competitors, and your mind.** No two golf courses are the same so your mind is always processing the course conditions, layout, types of grass, and green speed. Let's not forget about Mother Nature either—unlike in some sports, you must worry about the weather, temperature, and wind every single round. The competition is also fierce at all levels.
- **Golf is an individual sport.** Since it's a solo sport, the results are all on you and there are no teammates to blame if things go bad and no one is coming to save you during those tough rounds. When things are looking bad, it's easy to feel like you're Tom Hanks in the movie *Cast Away*, stranded on an island, searching desperately for answers, and talking to a white ball, trying to figure out how to survive. However, when things are good, there's only one person responsible for long drives, beautiful iron shots, great short game and hot putter—YOU. That's why it's so wildly rewarding when you put it all together and score well.

All of these reasons are why it's so taxing on your mind. Luckily, the brain is malleable, meaning you can influence, train, and learn to control it with practice. The problem is that most of us don't learn these concepts in school and must learn them independently.

In this section, you will learn simple but effective strategies to upgrade your mind and master the mental side of golf. As you will see in this book, the mind is a powerful tool once you learn how to use it to your advantage.

1. Cultivate an Attitude of Gratitude

◆

Your attitude is everything on the golf course (and in life). So many players have a bad attitude on the links and wonder why they don't score like they want. To play better golf and set yourself up for a better mental game, **change your attitude to gratitude.**

Being grateful is something you control and can have a massive impact on your golf game. Here's what *Harvard Health* said about the power of gratitude:

"In positive psychology research, gratitude is strongly and consistently associated with greater happiness. Gratitude helps people feel more positive emotions, relish good experiences, improve their health, deal with adversity, and build strong relationships."

Gratitude equals happiness.

If you're happier on the golf course, you won't get as frustrated or emotional, enjoy good shots more, feel better during and after the round, have the mental strength to deal with bad shots, and create better relationships with fellow players. All these positive results by simply choosing to be grateful.

Think about it like this...

You're lucky enough to have money to own golf clubs and pay for green fees. You're healthy enough to be able to swing a golf club at high speeds and hit shots your former self could never imagine. And you're fortunate enough to live in a place where golf courses are widely available for you to play. Some people don't have these things in life but want them deeply.

You do, so appreciate them immediately.

I know so many golfers who play golf like it's a job they hate and have zero fun. Even though they have no aspirations of playing golf for a living, they make each shot and each round seem like it is life or death.

Playing with so much stress and pressure usually makes your performance worse. Anytime you expect too much from your game or want to shoot a certain number, it almost never happens.

Instead of trying to force good golf and make each shot seem like your life is on the line, change your perspective.

Play golf with an attitude of gratitude.

Here's how; be grateful that you woke up today and made it safely to the golf course. That you got to play with friends or family (or had the chance to meet new people). Be grateful that your body allows you to swing a heavy, awkward club at high speeds to chase a golf ball all over the course.

Be grateful for everything in your life—on or off the golf course.

I know it sounds corny, but it's true. It's so easy to get caught up in the day-to-day activities of life. We don't step back and appreciate all that we have, including the ability to play the greatest sport ever.

This single mindset shift can change how you play on the golf course. It can make your good days great and make the bad days a lot more enjoyable (but let's get real, there are no truly bad days on the golf course).

When you play with an attitude of gratitude, you learn to accept bad shots and appreciate good shots. You learn to…

- Swing with more freedom and fewer expectations.
- Enjoy the moment and not stress over a short putt you missed.
- Cherish the memories that golf allows you to create with incredible people.

For 99.9% of the golf population, it's a game and most of us aren't playing for our livelihood. Remember that when you hit a bad shot, it doesn't mean you can't pay the rent and feed your family.

Too many golfers put so much pressure on themselves to hit perfect golf shots, despite working a full-time job and not practicing enough, somehow thinking that expectations will somehow make you play better (newsflash—expectations like this will never help your score). As Tony Robbins said, *"Trade your expectations for appreciation and the world changes instantly."*

You can't control a lot in golf, but you can control your attitude. The sooner you appreciate every time you're on the golf course, the more you will invite greatness into your game.

2. Focus on What You Want

Once your attitude is right, the next step is creating a plan for every swing. As Jack Nicklaus said, *"I never hit a shot, not even in practice, without having a very sharp, in-focus picture of it in my head."*

Yet, most golfers think about what they *don't* to happen on each shot more than what they do want. Here's a perfect example.

I used to play a golf course where a water hazard ran the entire length of the 480 yard, par 4 18th hole. The pond came into play on the drive and on your approach shot, it was just staring you down the entire time and collected some of my golf balls too. It was a good challenge for your final hole.

Time and time again, I saw golfers who knew they needed a par (or even bogey) to log a personal best on the course. Then, out of nowhere, they would snipe hook their drive left or chunk an approach shot in the water by the green. Instead of carding a par, they walked away with bogeys, doubles, or worse.

Suddenly, a good day was ruined on the 18th hole. Sure, some of this is expected as it's a difficult hole and bad shots are part of the game. But I noticed these uncharacteristically bad swings even when they hadn't missed on the left side all day. It was as if they suddenly developed a snipe hook walking from the 17th green to the 18th tee. You might have witnessed this on a golf course you play frequently.

Why do so many golfers hit terrible shots at the worst possible moments? Sure, the golf swing plays a role, but often, there's something much bigger at play.

The answer: your subconscious mind.

Here's the thing; when golfers see a deep bunker, out of bounds or water like the hole I just mentioned, they usually think, *Don't hit it there*. The problem is that the subconscious mind doesn't understand negative statements.

For example, when you say to yourself, *Don't hit out of bounds*, your mind processes that thought as ~~Don't~~ *Hit it out of bounds.*

At that moment, before you ever take the club away to start your backswing, your mind is already working against you. While this doesn't mean you will naturally hit it where you *don't* want to every time you have this thought, it's not helping your scores. You're sabotaging yourself before you've even started your backswing.

Instead, you need to focus on what you want from the shot, not what you don't want.

Our minds want to help us achieve, but we need to send it the right message. Therefore, you need to focus on what you want - the fairway or green - instead of what you don't want from the shot.

Dr. Maxwell Maltz described the subconscious mind's role perfectly in his book, *Psycho-Cybernetics*. As he stated, *"When you see a thing clearly in your mind, your creative 'success mechanism' within you takes over and does the job much better than you could do it by conscious effort or willpower."*

Your mind *wants* to help you succeed and achieve your goals. But it's up to you to give it a clear picture of what you want to achieve with each swing or putt. Not what you don't want!

Most golfers don't understand this concept and instead try to direct their conscious minds to hit a better shot. Instead of swinging freely, your mind is thinking about where not to hit it, as opposed to where you want the ball to go. And as Dr. Maltz said, your success mechanism, aka your subconscious, *"Does the job much better than you could do it by conscious effort or willpower."*

Don't get me wrong; it's okay to identify where you don't want the ball to go. But that shouldn't be the last thing you think about as it will give mixed signals to your success mechanism.

Here is an example of how I use this mental hack for an approach shot on the golf course.

- First, I use my rangefinder to get the distance to the flag and pick a target for my ideal shot. Sometimes it's the flag; other times, it's the middle part of the green.
- Then I scan the green and think about where to miss and where not to miss. Remember, golf is a game of misses.
- Then I decide on the shot I intend to hit and pick the club that will give it the best chances of making it happen.
- Finally, I go through my pre-shot routine and focus solely on my target before pulling the trigger.

During my pre-shot routine, I am not saying to myself, "Don't hit in the water," or, "Don't miss left."

Instead, I am focusing all my energy on where I want the ball to go. This doesn't mean you will never hit it OB or in a hazard again, but at least you won't sabotage your success before ever swinging the club.

Always focus on what you want from the shot, not what you don't want.

3. Reframe Nerves to Minimize First Tee Jitters

First tee jitters are real and one part of the game that makes golf so mentally challenging.

To see good golfers hit bad shots, head to the first tee and watch a few groups. Whether you're a 20 handicap at a local course or a PGA Tour pro playing in the Ryder Cup, everyone has butterflies on the first hole. Sometimes, bad shots can occur from over-excitement.

I'm not here to judge, as I've hit some awful first tee shots myself. The worst first tee shot I've ever hit was in a college tryout where I dead-topped my drive into a creek ... with the coach and entire team watching. It was one moment where my soul wanted to leave my body just to end the embarrassment.

To this day, it was truly one of the worst shots in my life. It felt like my life was over and like I would never overcome the horrific shot. But looking back, I'm glad it happened because I played for that same college for two years after a successful open tryout. I overcame my nerves and qualified in two college tryouts to earn a spot on the team (I had to qualify again after being a red-shirt my first year). It took a lot of mental strength to overcome that bad memory and not until a decade later did I learn how to reframe my nerves.

Even now, 20 plus years later of playing golf, I still get the first tee jitters. Everyone gets those butterflies—yes, even Tiger Woods. I remember hearing him say in an interview that, despite all his wins and accomplishments, he still feels those butterflies flying around in his stomach. Tiger explained that he thinks you *should* feel them too because it means you care enough about the game.

Instead of trying to fight them and wish they weren't there, accept that they are part of the game. If you feel butterflies and some nervous energy, it means you're excited about golf and want to be there. It means you are passionate about your game and want to perform; they aren't a bad thing.

The key is to get those butterflies flying together.

You want to lean into your nervous feelings and reframe them as excitement because you probably are both nervous and excited, which is a good thing. You need to trick your brain into being excited, not nervous, which is easy.

Your brain doesn't understand the difference between being nervous or excited. With both states, your blood pressure rises, the heart beats faster, and you have increased alertness.

So when you're nervous, say to yourself, "I am excited. I am excited. I am excited." This will help your brain feel at ease and adjust your mindset so that you're using these feelings to hit a good shot on the first hole!

Remember, there is no biological difference between the two states. It's all about reframing to get excited about the opportunity.

Other ways to help ease your nerves on the first tee:

- Commit to a target.
- Take several deep breaths.
- Go through your pre-shot routine.
- Hit the last shot on the range with the club you will use on the first tee.

After you reframe your mindset, swing with confidence. Then find it and go hit your second shot of the day.

The first shot doesn't matter as much as you think. I've hit great first drives and made bogey or worse. Conversely, I've hit awful drives and made birdies and pars. That's just golf—don't let a little nervous excitement hinder a great first swing.

You got this!

🎙 PODCAST Episode:

To learn more about overcoming first tee jitters, listen to the episode on first tee jitters on the Wicked Smart Golf Podcast.
Visit www.wickedsmartgolf.com/book to listen now.

4. Write on Your Glove

Perspective is everything in golf and another part of the mental game you control. As Dr. Wayne Dyer said, *"If you change the way you look at things, the things you look at change."*

So many players struggle with the mental side of things because they expect so much from their games. We seem to think we should hit every shot perfectly, make every putt, and play seemingly perfect golf. But that's just not possible, and if it was, then no one would play golf as it would be too easy.

Before going to Q-school pre-qualifying in 2019, I worked with a sports psychologist for a few sessions to make sure I was 100% ready for the biggest competition of my life. While I learned a ton working together, one trick was so simple and practical that I have to share it with you.

To keep things in perspective for Q-school, he told me to write the numbers "2, 3, 4, 5" on my glove. He said, *"If you make a 2, 3, 4, or 5, don't complain and accept it. That's all you need to make the cut and advance to the next stage."*

It was a rule I couldn't react if I made a 2-5 on any holes. So I wrote it on my glove and it helped me keep everything in perspective, despite all the pressure of the event. When I missed a birdie putt but still made a four on the hole, my glove reminded me that anything from a 2 to a 5 will not get me in trouble.

A subtle reminder like this is a good way to stay present and keep your head in the round. Visual cues are a great way to stay present, not overreact to any one shot or hole, and maintain a positive attitude in the round.

5. Keep Breathing

◆

Your breathing patterns are a signal to your brain about what's going on in the real world. If you're taking big, deep breaths, your mind is calm and everything is okay. But if you're taking shallow breaths, a lot of bad things happen as your mind starts to go into panic mode. An article in *Headspace* found,

"Shallow breathing can turn into panic attacks, cause dry mouth and fatigue, aggravate respiratory problems, and is a precursor for cardiovascular issues. This breathing pattern also creates tension in other parts of the body and can lead to a lot of everyday problems."

The last thing you want is tension and excess stress when playing golf. Plus, shallow breathing puts your mind into fight-or-flight mode unintentionally.

For example, when you're nervous before a round, you're likely to stop taking normal deep breaths. Unfortunately, your brain takes this as a warning signal that your life is in danger and reacts negatively. Therefore, it's so important to keep breathing throughout the round.

You want to constantly supply your brain with plenty of oxygen to stay calm and collected. This will help you reduce tension, sharpen your focus, and minimize negative emotions that inevitably happen in golf.

If you hit a poor shot and react, it's even more important to take a deep breath. Remind your brain that everything is okay and that you can relax. As Byron Nelson said, *"One way to break up any kind of tension is good deep breathing."*

Before the first tee-off, take a few deep breaths to let your mind know that everything is okay. After a bad shot or bad hole, take a few deep breaths and before a difficult shot, take a few deep breaths too.

Make a conscious effort to keep breathing to reduce tension and stress and play your best golf.

6. Change Your Body Language

It's been said that your body language is more powerful than words.

When I was in high school, I had horrible body language on the golf course. When my parents came to watch me compete, they could look at my body language and know if I was playing well or badly. My competitors could see it too.

But now, I could be +7 or -5 on the round and my body language won't change, mostly. I am still human. Because now, I understand that the way you move your body plays a big role in your overall confidence and how you swing.

What does your body language reflect on the golf course? Does it signal that you're doing well or that you're counting down the holes until you finish the round and can forget about golf?

Fortunately, you control your body language. Your body signals to your mind your mood and attitude, so make sure it's sending the right message.

You want to avoid negative body language like:

- Avoiding eye contact
- Having your head down
- Tense facial expressions
- Arms folded in front of body

Instead, focus on more effective body language like:

- Smile
- Chin up
- Eye contact
- Upright and open posture

Think about it; if you're walking with your head down and shoulders slumped, you're not setting yourself up for success with the next swing. You're signaling defeat to the Golf Gods and they won't have mercy on your bad attitude.

But if you're walking with your chin, shoulders, and chest up, it signals confidence in yourself. It signals to your mind, *The round isn't over and I can still finish strong.* Think back to the first lesson - be grateful that you're even out playing golf for a quick mindset shift.

While there are a lot of ways to improve your body language, I would argue that the most important aspect in golf is to keep your head up. Don't put your head down and dwell on a bad shot or bad hole.

Keep your head and eyes up to appreciate the views and the fact that you're lucky enough to play golf. Scott Fawcett, the creator of Decades Golf, describes it as *"Eyes on the horizon"* which I think is a perfect representation of strong body language in a player.

Even if you're hitting it badly and are disappointed with the results, manage your body language. This is especially important in tournaments when you're competing against others. Don't let them see you struggle as you will give them a mental advantage.

7. Watch Your Self-Talk

◆

Another aspect of the mental game you control is your self-talk. Once your body language is under control, the next thing to do is check your language patterns.

What you say to yourself can build you up or tear you down. Golf is already hard enough; don't make it more difficult by speaking badly of yourself. As *Psychology Today* said,

"The content of your self-talk is important because, believe it or not, you are the most influential person, in your head. Yes, other people can certainly influence the way we feel and think, but at the end of the day, we are the ones who accept or reject the messages received from others."

Not to mention, your mind loves to make what you say about yourself come true, regardless of if it's positive or negative. That's why it's so significant to speak about positive things in your life (on or off the golf course).

What you say to yourself during the round plays a pivotal role in playing your best golf.

Just like my body language, my self-talk used to be horrible and negative. I would say things like:

- *"I'm a terrible putter."*
- *"Just not my day on the greens."*
- *"What did I do to deserve all this bad luck?"*
- *"My warm-up was terrible, so I better have my short game today."*

The woe is me mentality never helped my game. It wasn't until I went on my development journey in 2016-2018 that I learned the power of the words you speak. I learned to retrain my self-talk with conscious effort, and now people call me the most optimistic player they know, which is a huge compliment because golf requires an insane amount of optimism and positivity to get the most out of your game.

Now, when I'm playing with new people, I can figure their game out in two holes based on self-talk and body language. It cracks me up when someone misses a few putts on the first few holes and says, *"Just not my day today,"* or when a fellow player complains about the course conditions. It's like they think whining to the Golf Gods will help them when they're just setting themselves up for more of the same results.

Your self-talk is a choice you must make. What you say to yourself (both internally and externally) determines how much fun you have and how well you can play in any round. Don't forget, your mind is always listening to what you're saying, so make sure it's hearing positive, empowering statements, not negative ones.

To change your self-talk, you must first become aware of your language now. The next time you tee it up, focus solely on what you say out loud to your playing partners and under your breath to yourself. If you're like most golfers, you will be shocked about how many negative things you say to yourself without even realizing it.

But you hopefully will notice you say some positive things too. When you notice that, congratulate yourself when you say positive, empowering statements. Then try to catch yourself when you're spewing negative venom, so you catch yourself in the act. If you have nothing positive to say, keep quiet. It's better to stay neutral than berate yourself and your abilities on the golf course.

A good rule is, if you wouldn't say it to one of your playing partners, you should never say it to yourself. Treat yourself just like you do another person!

You must maintain a positive, optimistic attitude throughout the round.

As Bill Pennington said in *On Par,* *"Central to being a golfer is the belief that you will get better. Golf is so routinely humiliating that if we didn't know we were going to improve, it's doubtful we could press on."*

Control what you can by speaking to yourself like your own hype man. Become your own biggest fan on the golf course (and in life).

🎙 PODCAST Episode:

To learn more about improving your self-talk, listen to the episode on Wicked Smart Golf Podcast.
Visit www.wickedsmartgolf.com/book to listen now.

8. Try Out Neutral Thinking

Imagine hitting a terrible shot, I mean terrible. Like topping it off the first shot in your college tryout bad or shanking an iron on the 18th hole after a good round.

Then, imagine someone in your group saying, *"Just stay positive."* If you're like me, the last thing you want to do is think positive when you just hit an awful golf shot.

Don't get me wrong; positive thinking is good in theory. But if someone tells me to stay positive after I just hit a shank, I want to tomahawk throw my golf club at them. Sometimes staying positive sounds impossible when you're as angry as the Hulk.

Luckily, there's an alternative to positive thinking that can help you manage your emotions... It's called **neutral thinking**. I first learned about this from Trevor Moawad, who has coached NFL stars to Navy SEALs and CEOs. As he said in the book *Getting to Neutral*:

"There comes a point where being neutral is the only option. You have to go to that place, because otherwise it's impossible to get clarity and calm things down. I love the idea of taking a moment to pause and then going to neutral."

Instead of making a bad shot worse and spiraling out of control, accept it for what it is. You can't change the past and the future hasn't happened yet. Instead of spiraling into an endless sea of negative thoughts, stay neutral in your thinking. Plus, has thinking negatively ever actually helped your game? My guess is no.

Instead of trying to think positively after a bad golf shot (which is a lot to ask for some players, myself included), stay neutral. Take a deep breath and don't make the situation worse with negative thinking. Take each shot one at a time and don't make things worse with negative thinking.

Like self-talk, body language, and breathing, this is 100% in your control. If you struggle with this, write something on your scorecard or glove to act as a visual cue to remember the power of neutral thinking.

9. Master Your Mind with Meditation

The mind doesn't get much of a break these days. When we wake up, we are bombarded with notifications, texts, emails and people wanting our attention. But sometimes, your mind needs a reset other than just sleeping at night. The best way to recharge your brain is to learn more about the power of meditation.

Maybe you've meditated, maybe you haven't. Maybe you think it's total BS or think it's the key to life. For years, I thought meditation was ridiculous and told myself I would never do it. But as I found more stress in my life, I needed something to help cope with the pressure of entrepreneurship and the quest of pursuing professional golf. It was that time I realized how many CEOs, athletes, and successful people use meditation to improve their mindset.

Here's the thing; if meditation works for Tiger Woods and Phil Mickelson, there's something to it. My thought process was that if it works for two of my golf idols and I want to improve, I should have the courage to learn more about it and try it out myself.

Tiger Woods learned meditation at an early age from his mother and has said how much of a staple it's been in his life. While Phil Mickelson learned how to meditate later in his career to stay focused throughout the round. Tiger has 15 major championships and Phil just won the PGA Championship at age 50, so meditation can help your mental game to win the biggest events in golf.

In my own life, I've learned to use both meditation and hypnosis to take control of my mind and emotions. It not only helps with golf but with all aspects of life. Since golf and life are eerily similar, this practice can help you in both areas.

Meditation is the gateway to the mind. When you learn how to meditate off the course, it will help you on the course by allowing you to stay calm, alert, and focused.

The cool thing is there is no "one way" to meditate. For some, it's sitting in a room silently for a few minutes. Other people use apps like Headspace or Primed Mind (both of which I recommend). Or you can attend a formal workshop to learn a form known as Transcendental Meditation (TM).

I've used all these methods and they've had a profound effect on my mental game. Like anything, it takes time to see results from your meditation practice. Just like changing your golf swing, it won't happen overnight, but it will pay off for the rest of your life.

You have to trust the process, not rush it. Don't forget, it's called "meditation practice" for a reason. Over time, it can give you the mental tools to help you deal with the stresses of life on or off the golf course. In golf, we need all the mental tools we can get to cope with the rollercoaster of emotions that the sport brings out.

To learn more about my favorite apps and tracks to start meditating, visit www.wickedsmartgolf.com/book now.

10. Visualize Success

Visualization is another one of the most powerful tools in your mental game toolbox. If you aren't visualizing success on the golf course, you're making things much harder on yourself. As Sir Nick Faldo said, *"Visualization is the most powerful thing we have."*

Seeing really is believing. Athletes in various sports tap into the power of visualization to help them achieve their goals.

So why does this mental training work so well?

A [Psychology Today article](#) summed it up perfectly:

"Brain studies now reveal that thoughts produce the same mental instructions as actions. Mental imagery impacts many cognitive processes in the brain: motor control, attention, perception, planning, and memory. So the brain is getting trained for actual performance during visualization. It's been found that mental practices can enhance motivation, increase confidence and self-efficacy, improve motor performance, prime your brain for success, and increase states of flow—all relevant to achieving your best life!"

When you visualize your success on the golf course, it's priming your mind for the future.

I like to think about visualizing as daydreaming with a purpose. The best part is that if you do it with enough repetition and enthusiasm, your brain will think it's real because your brain can't differentiate between what is real and what is imagined.

If you don't believe me, here is a good example. Think about grabbing a juicy lemon and biting into it like you would a slice of pizza. Chances are you imagine the texture of the peel, the sourness, and bitter taste... even though you didn't bite the lemon, you felt it in your body.

It's amazing how you can think about something and have the feelings as if it were happening. Instead of using visualization negatively, use it to train your brain for success in golf.

There are two ways specifically to use visualization in golf.

Off-Course Visualization

The first way to visualize success is when you're at home, away from the golf course. Sit in a quiet room with your eyes closed and imagine what you want to accomplish on the golf course, whether it's a certain move in your swing, shooting a specific score, or winning a tournament.

To make it even more effective, bring in your other senses to make it feel realistic to your mind. Imagine fist-pumping as you drain a putt on 18 to win a tournament. Imagine your teammates or friends saying, "Congratulations." Imagine the joy you feel holding the trophy.

Do this repeatedly so that when you're in pressure-packed moments, you're not as nervous. Your brain will think you have been there so often mentally, that it will feel more normal and keep your nerves at bay.

Another great way to use visualization is to write in a journal. Write about your ideal round, how you're swinging, your confidence, your attitude, how you're battling the conditions and playing great golf. Write in the past tense with statements like, "I hit it so pure today. My mental game was sharp, I didn't let my emotions get to me, and persevered through the tough shots." Writing in the past tense as if it's already done is a powerful way to trick your mind into thinking you are a great golfer.

Get clear in your mind to make it happen on the golf course.

On-Course Visualization

The other way to use visualization on the golf course is during your pre-shot routine. As I mentioned in an earlier chapter, it's essential to picture and imagine what you want to happen for a shot. You want to think and imagine a shot going on the green, not going in the water. You never want to say, "Don't hit it in the water." Instead, focus on what you want.

As you go through your pre-shot routine for any shot on the golf course, picture what you want to happen. For full swings, imagine a shot tracer of the perfect ball flight like you're watching golf on TV. For short chips and pitches, imagine the ball hitting your landing spot and releasing perfectly. With putting, imagine looking up and seeing the ball roll into the middle of the hole as you're reading the line.

Or, if you are someone who "feels" more than you see something, imagine feeling the ball launch off the face. Imagine the feeling of the ball coming off the putter face and feeling it in your hands.

Visualization is another part of your mental game you control and something that the best players in the world do consistently.

11. Manage Emotions

◆

Notice the title of this lesson is "Manage Emotions" not "Don't Get Mad." Because I'd be a huge hypocrite if I told you to never get mad and why we already covered the power of neutral thinking.

I'm not asking you to play golf like an emotionless robot; instead, I'm asking you to manage them so you don't let one bad shot affect future shots. It's okay to get a little upset after a bad shot if you can get over it quickly.

This quote from what Tiger Woods told his son Charlie about getting mad is everything,

"Son, I don't care how mad you get. Your head could blow off for all I care, just as long as you're 100% percent committed to the next shot. That next shot should be the most important shot in your life. It should be more important than breathing."

Unless you're an alien, golf will bring negative emotions occasionally. As I mentioned, this is something I struggled with in high school and still do to this day. But what's changed is my ability to manage my emotions quickly, so within 10-15 seconds, I'm over it and ready for the next shot.

A good trigger I use to manage my emotions is my golf glove. I usually say a few choice words out loud (or under my breath) after a poor shot. But once I take off my glove, my mind shifts to the next shot instead of dwelling on the past. The glove is a trigger to get over it and move on so I don't let one bad shot spiral my round out of control.

Get those negative emotions out of your system as fast as possible, and then commit 100% focus for your next shot. Do not let one bad shot compound into several bad shots (or bad holes) from not managing your emotions.

12. Be Your Own Biggest Fan

You must believe you're a better golfer than you are to reach your potential. You need to become your own biggest fan, even if you're miles away from achieving your golf goals.

Dr. Bob Rotella said it best. *"To be the best golfer you can be, you need to create your own story, your own reality, then do everything you can to fulfill it. Great storytelling can help you reach your goals."*

The mind works in mysterious ways, but one thing is for sure, success starts in your mind and then manifests in the real world. Think about how many things you've wanted to happen that you first vividly imagined.

Maybe it was landing a dream job, finding your perfect house, or getting into the best shape of your life. It all started with a thought and believing you could make it happen.

The same goes for golf.

Before I ever broke 80, I knew I had it in me and thought about it often. I knew I could become the type of golfer who always shoots in the 70s. With time and work, it's true and it takes a horrible day to finish in the 80s.

It doesn't happen overnight, but it will happen faster if you believe it. Don't let your friends, playing partners, or family get you down, either.

Believe in yourself and tell yourself positive things all the time - even when you're off the course. Only say things like, "My game is getting better" or "I'm really proud of my putting/driving/etc." The more you do it, the better and the sooner you will reap the rewards.

13. Stay Present

I don't know about you, but my mind loves to wander on the golf course. While meditation and other mindfulness techniques have helped, it's still something I must focus on during the round.

To play your best golf, you need to put a leash on your mind (metaphorically speaking) so you can focus on one thing only—*the present moment.* You will never play your best golf if you dwell on bad shots you hit earlier in the day or get anxious about upcoming shots in the current round. As Dr. Joseph Parent said in *Zen Golf,* *"The past is history, the future is a mystery, being alive in this moment is a gift. That's why they call it the present."*

You can't change the past and the future hasn't happened yet. Focus 100% of your attention on the present moment to give yourself the best chance to hit a good shot.

Another easy trick to stay present is to wear a rubber band on your wrist. Anytime you look back to a putt you wish you made or a future shot you're anxious about hitting, snap it. This is another great trick I learned from a sports psychologist that has done wonders for me on the golf course.

As I like to say, snap back to reality!

Over time, this will train your mind to stay more focused on the present moment and not drift to the past or future. Always remember, golf is one shot at a time - don't get ahead of yourself.

14. Create a Memory Bank of Good Shots

Did you know you're more likely to remember bad shots than good shots? It's called **negativity bias** and means that your brain is hardwired for negativity.

Here's a formal explanation from *Very Well Mind*:

"Our tendency to pay more attention to bad things and overlook good things is likely a result of evolution. Earlier in human history, paying attention to bad, dangerous, and negative threats in the world was literally a matter of life and death. Those who were more attuned to danger and who paid more attention to the bad things around them were more likely to survive."

But golf is not life or death. You no longer need to pay attention to danger to survive, especially if you're playing golf!

You need to train your memory to forget bad shots quickly and remember positive shots as much as possible. This is easier said than done because the mind is wired for negativity, but it is possible.

Here's how I train my brain with good and bad shots.

For bad shots, I try to limit my emotions as much as possible. Not because I don't care or because I've reached some monk's next level of awareness. Not at all—I still want to slam and throw clubs as much as ever. I just choose not to for one main reason.

The more emotional you get, the more likely a memory will stick with you.

Rewind to my college tryout, where I topped my first tee shot in front of the coach and entire team. I had so many negative emotions and relived that situation for weeks, if not months afterward. I nearly developed

PTSD from that one golf shot. While it was a bad shot, I made it worse by getting mad, emotional and ingraining it into my subconscious.

Plus, don't forget about negativity bias and how the mind remembers negative events much more than positive ones. That's why it is so important to minimize your emotions, so you don't put your brain on high alert and make it more likely to remember a specific bad shot.

I also try to laugh it off, so my brain realizes we're not in danger and everything is okay. Then I concentrate on the next shot with 100% focus. I save analyzing the shot for after the round, never during it.

For good shots, I do the exact opposite because I know it's harder for my mind to remember good shots. I'm not afraid to tell everyone while the ball is in flight how good I hit it. I'll fist pump a clutch putt, mentally pat myself on the back, and use positive self-talk after a good hole. Not in a bragging sort of way, but to remind myself about the good shots and fight the negativity bias.

Then I relive it often after the round. This will give the memory a better chance to stay with me so I can use it when I need a confidence boost in the future.

Finally, I use the Notes App to act as a golf tracker to remember epic shots. After each round, I make sure I notate and detail them as much as possible to have a memory bank of my best shots. These are great to lean on when you're on the course and facing a tough shot.

Remember, you need to constantly remind yourself about the good shots because our minds are wired for negativity.

Plus, forgetting bad shots on the course is a gift. The best example of this is Dustin Johnson. Even if he hits a horrible shot, he never seems fazed and can get up to the next one without a care in the world.

Brooks Koepka even called DJ a goldfish once in a press conference. While it's easy to take that as a negative statement, it's a compliment. Goldfish are notorious for having one of the shortest memories of any living species (about seven seconds), which is what you need on the golf course.

So when you hit a bad shot, forget about it like a goldfish to rid yourself of that negative memory. It's not the first and not the last bad shot you will hit in your golf career. Move on to the next one and minimize emotions to not let it compound into more bad shots.

15. Never Give Up

◆

The last piece of mental advice is simple—don't quit. Not on the round, not on any hole, or on any shot that happens on any golf course.

As Tiger Woods said, *"The days you don't have it, you don't mail it in, you don't pack it in. You give it everything you got and you grind it out."*

Because Tiger knows it's not over until it's over.

For example, I can't tell you how often I've hit three awful shots on a par 4, only to make a 30-foot putt to save par. Or I've started off bogey, bogey and shot under par by the time I finished the 18th hole.

While it's important never to give up on a hole, it's also important never to give up on the round either. After competing in endless tournaments, I find it astonishing how many people quit in the middle of a one-day qualifier or don't show up the next day after carding a bad first round in a multiple-day event.

Here's the thing… *Who cares if you post a high score? Who cares what other people think about your golf game?*

I would rather post an 84 as a scratch golfer than see a WD next to my name on the scoreboard. You never know what will happen if you quit, and you must live with that regret.

Think about it; what if you quit after a bad nine but would've come back and shot your best back nine ever? What if you made a double eagle or a hole in one?

It's golf; you just never know. You must expect yourself to have the ability to hit great shots and turn a bad day around at any given moment.

Here's a perfect example that happened as I got back into tournament golf.

In my first US Open local qualifier in 2017, I played poorly on the front nine. You need to shoot minimum -4 to make it to the next qualifier to give some context. The course is difficult for these events—usually tipped out at 7,200+ yards, with firm/fast greens, and the pins are tucked in the hardest locations.

After eight holes, I was eight over par and frankly embarrassed with my performance. My bogeys weren't intimidating my playing partners and I wasn't thinking about booking my flight for the next qualifying site.

As we walked off the 9th tee, a guy in my group (a well-established player in Arizona) hinted that I should quit after the next hole. He did it without telling me to quit, instead offering a short story as we approached the green.

This memory is burned into my brain. He casually said, *"I remember once I was five over after nine one year. I knew I wasn't going to make it, so I bought my caddy an early lunch and apologized for making him come out today."*

I couldn't tell if it was an insult or not, but I took it as one. For a millisecond, I thought about walking off as I wasn't going to advance to the next stage.

But then I thought, *No way, I paid two hundred dollars for this round of golf, I will finish it.* Plus, I've never been a quitter in my whole life, and my first US Open qualifier wasn't the time to start.

I made a solid par on the 9th hole and my mindset shifted instantly on the 10th tee, and I snapped back to my normal golf. I ended up shooting a few over on the back nine, but my game was 10X better.

While I didn't get anywhere near close to qualifying, I proved that I can score near par at a US Open qualifying venue. Plus, I reminded my subconscious that I can turn it around no matter how badly the front nine goes.

Sure, I had a bad front nine, but a great turnaround gave me loads of confidence for the future. Confidence that wouldn't have happened if I walked off the green as my playing partner suggested.

Ironically, four years later, I got paired up with the same guy, at the same course, for the same US Open qualifier. Seriously, you can't make this stuff up. While I'd love to tell you I played the round of my life and advanced to the next stage to prove him wrong, it didn't happen.

However, the next best solution did happen that fateful day the Golf Gods provided.

That same guy who told me to quit four years previously dunked two balls in the water on the 9th hole. A mini-meltdown ensued; he knew he would not advance, so he handed me his scorecard and walked off the course.

Even though he quit after the front nine, I still beat him for the first half of the round and got the last laugh. It was a full-circle moment and one I'll never forget.

The lesson here is that bad rounds will happen, that's just how golf works!

If you quit, you never give yourself a chance to make an epic comeback you will have in your memory bank forever. Plus, quitting in golf can bleed into other areas of your life too.

As Arnold Palmer said, *"I've always made a total effort, even when the odds seemed entirely against me. I never quit trying; I never felt that I didn't have a chance to win."*

Just remember, quitting is NOT an option. Always stay in the fight.

Because once a quitter, always a quitter.

Bonus Video

Don't forget to watch the bonus materials at www.wickedsmartgolf.com/book to recap mental game mastery.

Section II: Practice Like a Pro

Learn how to make your practice routines more efficient to take your game from the range to the golf course

Practice makes perfect… *Right?*

Wrong.

There is no such thing as perfect in sports, especially for playing golf. The problem is that most golfers chase the perfect swing, thinking it will somehow lead to lower scores. Trust me, it doesn't guarantee low scores every round.

The perfect swing does not exist. Sure, the best players in the world share a lot of common moves in their swing, but no two players have the same exact swing. Plus, even if you get your swing figured out for a while, it's always fluid and changing.

Most golfers practice by going to the driving range, hitting tons of golf balls, and hope they walk away better. Sometimes they do, but a week, month, or year later, there's always something new to improve in your swing. Other times, they leave the golf course wondering why they even bothered with practice.

I've been there myself countless times. There is nothing more frustrating than spending time and money on the range only to walk away feeling worse about your game.

It's time to change that, so you never walk away feeling defeated again. Before diving into the best ways to practice like a professional, let's first talk about some common mistakes to avoid.

7 Biggest Practice Mistakes Most Golfers Make

In most sports, practice leads to real change - the more you practice, the more it shows up in competition.

In basketball, running more will give you the endurance to help you last longer in the game without needing rest. While working on free throws time and time again in practice makes you nearly automatic when the game is on the line. The same in soccer, football, and every other sport.

But golf differs from most sports in terms of more practice relating to more success. As Harvey Penick said in his book, *For All Who Love the Game,*

"Every day I see golfers out there banging away at bucket after bucket. If I ask them what they're doing, they say, 'What does it look like I'm doing, Harvey? I'm practicing!' Well, they're getting exercise all right. But few of them are really practicing."

If you're like most golfers, I'm sure you can relate. We all are guilty of exercise vs. practice sometimes. But to get the most out of your game and reach your potential, you need to learn how to practice effectively and efficiently.

Here are seven of the biggest practice mistakes to avoid.

Not Practicing Enough

The first mistake is that some golfers don't practice enough (or at all) and then wonder why they aren't shooting better scores. While "more" practice isn't always the answer, of course, you still must put in some work behind the scenes to shine on the golf course. As Dr. Bob Rotella said, *"A golfer has to train his swing on the practice tee, then trust it on the course."*

To master any new skill or sport, you need to put in the reps to get the most out of your game. As Malcolm Gladwell said in the book *Outliers*, *"It takes 10,000 hours of deliberate practice to become an expert."* While practice doesn't make perfect (because let's get real, perfect doesn't exist in golf), practice does make permanent.

To play your best golf, you need to train your swing enough in practice to have confidence on the course. Don't expect to shoot your best scores if you don't know your swing and haven't put in the work behind the scenes to deserve lower scores.

Not Using an Alignment Aid or Picking a Target

The second mistake most golfers make is not using an alignment aid or picking a target on the range. Instead, most golfers just bang ball after ball without checking their alignment or going toward a specific target.

This is a huge problem because it's how you ingrain bad habits without even realizing it, which is why you can leave the range feeling defeated and hopeless.

For example, one thing I notice is so many golfers aim right of the target but think they're set up perfectly.

Here's the problem…

Consciously, they don't realize they're aimed right, but their mind realizes the mistake. To compensate, their mind will help them try to pull the club to the left toward their original target. This results in the dreaded over-the-top move that produces pulls, slices, and pop-ups from getting too steep on the downswing.

You can avoid this costly mistake with an alignment stick(s) on most shots you hit on the range. After five to 10 warm-up balls with wedges, immediately use alignment sticks to ensure no bad habits accidentally creep into your swing.

Once you use alignment sticks, don't forget to always pick a target for each shot. So many golfers never pick a target (or they pick a broad general area), making it hard to measure whether you hit it well. Instead, pick a target and use your alignment sticks to ensure you have the proper setup for success.

If you want to be an overachiever, visualize each shot before hitting it like Jack "The Golden Bear" Nicklaus always did. Remember from the first section; focus on what you want with each shot and use the power of visualization to train your mind to get the results you want.

Target + Alignment + Visualization = Practicing with Purpose.

Thinking a Jumbo Bucket Will Solve Everything

The third mistake that most golfers make is hitting too many range balls. Like the second practice mistake, this can unconsciously create bad habits and hurt your game. Remember, golf is not like other sports and hitting too many golf balls can be counterproductive as you get tired, lazy, and develop bad habits.

The quality of practice is more important than the quantity of practice.

I would much rather see golfers hit a small bucket on the range and hit each shot with intention than rapid-fire a jumbo bucket. Plus, you will save money and avoid injuries by choosing a smaller bucket of golf balls. Remember, you don't get any bonus points from the Golf Gods for hitting more golf balls.

Don't get me wrong; sometimes you might need a longer practice session but not every time you practice. For example, if you're working on a specific new part of your swing, working with a coach or creating a new habit with a training aid, this is when you need more swings as repetition is how you retrain your subconscious mind and create new habits.

But you rarely need to hit as many golf balls as you think. As you'll learn in this book, extra time hitting balls could be much better spent on other areas of your game (like short game) that will yield better results.

Hitting Too Many Irons

I'm not sure why, but most golfers seem to think they must hit tons of iron repeatedly to become a good player. But if you look at your stats on an average round, I bet you'll see that most shots aren't with mid-to-long irons. Those clubs are only used a handful of times, yet most golfers are programmed to hit seven irons until the grooves wear down on the driving range. This isn't an effective way to spend your precious time!

So what's the answer?

Work on the shots that matter—specifically, what happens inside 125 yards. Mastering this part of your game is huge because it will let you take advantage of good drives for better looks at birdie and it will also help you recover from bad drives.

When your wedges, chipping/pitching and putting are sharp, you can still put together a solid score which is the epitome of playing wicked smart golf. I know first-hand as I was a terrible ball-striker in high school but managed to scrap it around thanks to a solid short game. Stop hitting so many irons on the range and instead, spend time with wedges and short irons.

Never Playing Practice Holes

Another huge mistake that too many players make is only using the range for drills instead of *"practice playing."*

Practice playing is using your imagination to play holes on the driving range as if you're on the golf course. Instead of just rapid-fire hitting golf balls like most struggling golfers, this practice method is a great way to work on your routine and hit an array of golf shots. This will keep your mind and body guessing and prepare you much more for the golf course.

For example, if hole #1 is a 420-yard par 4, hit the tee shot you would normally try to hit on the hole. Pick targets, create a fairway between two posts or trees, go through your full pre-shot routine, and execute as if you're on the course.

Then play the next shot based on your tee off. If you sprayed it right and would normally be under trees, hit a punch shot to get back into play or roll one onto the green. Practice playing will help your shot-making abilities and save you shots when you head to the course.

This type of practice on the range is so much more productive because you'll never hit the same shot twice. It keeps your mind and body guessing, so it feels natural when you're on the course to see the shot and then pull it off. Plus, it will help your imagination.

Remember, one habit of highly successful golfers is using imagination and visualization to play better golf. Even if you aren't doing it much now, practicing on the range will make it easier to take it to the course with you.

Ignoring Your Pre-Shot Routine

As you will soon learn in this book, the pre-shot routine is one of the most important pieces of a good golf swing. As Dave Pelz said in his book *Dave Pelz's Short Game Bible*, *"A good pre-shot ritual gives your subconscious a countdown which lets every part of your body know when things are going to happen."*

Aside from the emphasis on a good setup position, it's probably the only thing that all PGA Tour players and elite amateur golfers have in common. Even though no two players usually have the same pre-shot routine, every good player has their own version. It's how they get comfortable over each shot and give themselves the best chances to hit the shot they imagined.

Yet, most everyday golfers don't have a pre-shot routine. Or if they do, it seems to change a little every round and doesn't help them with their confidence on the course.

The reason a pre-shot routine is necessary is that it can help you build confidence for each shot (even the hard ones). It can also help you calm your nerves and hit each shot with maximum confidence.

A good pre-shot routine will also help you speed up play, minimize doubts, play better in tournaments, and score better consistently. But to reap these benefits, you need to practice it first on the range so it becomes second nature on the golf course. More on creating a pre-shot routine in this section.

Skipping Short Game and Putting

The final mistake so many players make is ignoring their short game and putting.

So many players skip this part of their game and wonder why they aren't shooting lower scores. I can't tell you how often I go to practice and see almost everyone on the range and no one on the putting or chipping green. It drives me crazy, but I understand why… For most golfers, hitting full shots feels like more fun than hanging out at the short game area.

But growing up, I was the opposite and learned to love short game practice (and still do). When I first got serious about golf at 13-14 years old, I barely hit it 200 yards off the tee, so I had to develop a strong short game or I'd never score well. Once I hit it longer, I had an awesome short game that helped me score extremely well.

Here's the thing; your swing isn't always going to be there… Some days, no matter how hard you try, your ball striking just will not show up. It even happens on the PGA Tour pros, so why should you expect it to be any different?

Therefore, you need a world-class short game to play consistent golf. The swing is simpler and easier to get right often. Rarely does a good short game just leave you like your full swing. The better your short game the better you'll score every single round.

If your long game is there that day, you can go low. And if your long game seems to take a day off, your short game can help you salvage your score.

Like any part of your game, you need to train it on the chipping/putting green to get results on the course. The good thing is that improving your short game is a lot easier than working on your full swing (which is a lifelong learning process). Instead, 15–30 minutes, even just a few times a week, at the short game area can make a big difference in your game.

Now that we've got the biggest practice mistakes out of the way, let's get into how to practice like a professional. As Tony Robbins said, *"Success always leaves clues"* and the best players in the world leave a lot of clues for how to get better; you just must know what to look for.

Here are the best ways to practice with purpose and make the most of each session. Some drills you might have heard of, while others might be brand new. I suggest keeping an open mind and remembering these are all proven ways to move your game forward.

16. Practice with a Plan

◆

To practice like a pro, you need to have a plan of action.

Think about it like this…

How often have you gone to the gym *without* a plan for what muscles you're working on, or how long the session will last only to have a mediocre workout where you spend more time scrolling your phone instead of sweating and putting in the reps? If you're like most people, it probably happens more than you care to admit—I've made this mistake too often myself.

Conversely, imagine when you go into the gym with a clear plan of action, how much better is your workout? If I have a plan like this, I know I will make the most of my workout:

- **Time**: 45 minutes
- **Muscle groups**: Chest and triceps
- **Exercises**: Four supersets and finish with push-ups until failure

With a plan like this, you will move from each exercise to another with focus and precision. You will leave the gym knowing you're one step closer to your fitness goals.

Golf is no different; whether you head to the driving range or the short game area, you need a plan of action to improve. Otherwise, you'll mindlessly hit shots and probably not move the needle on improving your golf game.

Intention is everything with practice.

As actor Jim Carrey pointed out in an interview, *"It's our intention. Our intention is everything. Nothing happens on this planet without it. Not one single thing has ever been accomplished without intention."*

A practice plan gives you the best chances to succeed by giving you clear intention. Showing up with a clear practice plan will keep you accountable and get you closer to hitting your goals. But it does not mean you'll improve every session or never walk away feeling frustrated. Let's get real; we're still talking about golf—the most difficult sport ever.

Here are some different practice plans to give you some inspiration on making the most of your time:

30-Minute Practice Plan

Remember, quality is more important than quantity. Even if you have 30 minutes, you can still get real results:

- **Short game only**: 10 minutes chipping (bump-n-runs), 10 minutes pitching/sand shots, 10 minutes putting drills.
- **Driving range only**: 5-minute warm-up, 10 minutes of drills, 15 minutes of "random" practice, aka hitting different shots every time (more on that coming up).

60-Minute Practice Plan

If you have a full hour to commit to your game, here are three practice routines to make the most of your time.

- **Short game only**: 15 minutes of short putts (3–6 feet), 15 minutes with a wedge/putter, seeing how many shots you can get up and down. Then head to the range, spend 30 minutes on wedges only.
- **Driving range only**: Warm up for 10 minutes and spend 20 minutes hitting balls with your full pre-shot routine. During the last half, you can do drills, skills practice, or play 9 on the driving range (more on that coming up).
- **Short and long game**: 30 minutes chipping, pitching, and putting before heading to the range (this will ensure you don't skip the most important part of your session). Then head to the range and work on technical swing changes or "random" practice for the other 30 minutes.
- **Three Clubs**: Spend 20 minutes with our driver, wedge, and putter as they are the most important clubs in the bag. In an average round, you probably use your driver at least 10 shots and it sets up your

approach shots. Your putter is used in every hole, and your favorite wedge is used often for approaches and scrambling around the green. This is why you should practice with these three clubs the most.

Again, these are just a few ideas to help you make the most out of your practice session. As you'll read throughout this section, there is no one way to practice. Each session is about spending time on your weaknesses, mastering your short game, and trying to simulate golf as if you were on the course.

17. Never Judge Your Practice Session on Time

◆

As I mentioned in the start of the chapter, one of the biggest mistakes so many golfers make is thinking that a longer session means a better session. But I want to repeat this lesson so you develop a new belief about time spent practicing. More time does not mean a better practice —I've gone to the range for 20 minutes and had breakthroughs, while I've gone for two hours and barely accomplished anything.

Don't get me wrong; *sometimes*, you do need longer sessions but not every time you want to practice. For example, if you just had a lesson and you're working on a new grip, takeaway, or some other part of your swing, a longer session could be more effective. When you're significantly changing your golf swing, you need more reps to normalize these changes.

But you don't need to spend hours and hours on the range every single time to get results. Sometimes you might need to "dig it out of the dirt" as Ben Hogan would say, but at other times 20 minutes is all you need. As Dr. Jim Afremow said in The Champion's Mind, *"The quality of your work in practice (input) determines your performance in competition (output). Just remember that it's not about how much practice time you put in; it's about what you put into the practice time."*

All it takes is one swing or one putt to have a breakthrough, and it doesn't mean you need to spend hours searching for it. I think this concept is even more important when it comes to putting. While you still need to work on your putting (specifically short putts), spending hours on the putting green doesn't guarantee results.

18. Develop a Tour Tempo

◆

Tempo is an interesting part of the game that doesn't get talked about enough. I always thought "low and slow" tempo was the key to success for the longest time. But as I got back into tournament golf and worked with Boyd Summerhays, I learned the importance of speeding up tempo.

Like most everyday golfers, my slow tempo was too slow, which led to a quick transition, inconsistent ball striking, and killed my total distance. When I learned how to speed up my tempo, my game improved almost overnight. While I promised to not go into any technical advice in this book, tempo is too important not to discuss.

Most amateurs need to speed up their tempo. For example, John Garrity wrote in the book, *Tour Tempo*:

"The great golfers have always swung more quickly and aggressively than middle and high handicappers. If you don't believe me, take a stopwatch and time a typical tour player's swing from takeaway to impact. The elapsed time will be between .93 seconds and 1.20 seconds, or about as long as it takes to flip a pancake."

He later said, "Now take that same stopwatch and time the swings of your average weekend golfer -- your 5 handicapper, your 15-handicapper, your can't-get-it-airborne 30-handicapper. You'll find that these nonprofessionals take anywhere from 1.3 seconds to a full 3.0 seconds to send the ball on its way."

If you want to play better golf, learn to swing faster when practicing on the driving range. Swinging with the old "low and slow" advice is a disaster for most everyday players. However, when I started swinging faster or smoother on the backswing, my distance increased, my ball striking improved, and my transition became noticeably better for my golf buddies.

When you're on the driving range working on swing changes, sometimes you need to slow it down to feel the changes. But most of the time, you should learn to speed up your swing like the best golfers in the world -

even if it terrifies you. The driving range is your time to test any theories, not the golf course, so take advantage of it.

To simplify, download the Tour Tempo app on your phone as it makes it simple to hear your way to a faster tempo. With the paid app, you can listen to tunes or commands that tell you when to take the club back, when to set the club at the top of your swing, and when you should finish your swing. It's one of the best investments you can make in your golf swing.

Start by going to the driving range with a buddy and time your current swing from start to finish. Then, work your way to get faster (but it will look smoother to the naked eye), so you're closer to the professional time of .93 to 1.20 seconds.

At first, it will feel awkward as ever, but after a few swings, your body will figure it out and adjust quickly. Over time, this app can have a huge impact on your game as long as you put in the reps on the driving range.

19. Record Your Swing (the Right Way)

◆

The camera on your phone can help you improve and shoot lower scores as much as any new golf club. Taking regular swing videos is one of the best practice tools and great for a few reasons.

First, recording your swing makes it easy to see how far you've come in your golf journey. Even when it feels like swing changes are taking forever, a quick glance at old videos should inspire you to keep going. I love looking back at videos from a year, three years, or even five years ago to see how much I've learned and how things have changed.

Second, your videos can help you get out of a slump. When things aren't going well, I'll look back at old videos when I was hitting it well to spot changes quickly. Therefore, it's important to record your swing when you're hitting it both well and badly. It makes it easier to self-assess your swing and make changes quickly to break out of a slump. Golf is all about knowing your swing, tendencies, and misses. Constantly getting videos is one of the best things to master your swing.

Even if you are among the small percentage of players that record their swing, there's a science to recording it the right way. The key is to make sure the camera is in the correct position so you can properly evaluate and analyze your swing videos. Unfortunately, most golfers get this wrong and it is something I did incorrectly for years and I still cringe when looking at old swing videos.

If you don't get the camera angle right, it's nearly impossible to analyze your swing and adjust. The wrong angles can lead to analyzing your swing incorrectly and then making incorrect swing changes, which only compounds your mistake… What a stupid game we play, right?

Invest in a cheap tripod on Amazon that collapses and easily fits in your golf bag to properly record your swing. Yes, it's a little weird at first when you whip out a tripod on the driving range and, yes, some other players will judge you. But I promise the good players will give you a silent nod of respect because you're one of the few players doing it right.

Once you get the tripod set up, you need to record with two angles to capture all parts of your swing. If you only get one angle, it's not as effective to properly analyze all aspects of your setup and swing.

Here are the two ways to record your golf swing:

Angle #1: Down the Line

This is the most common way to record your swing and likely what you see most golfers post on social media. A down-the-line angle makes it easy to evaluate your posture, takeaway, top of the swing, transition, and downswing. The problem is that most golfers have no consistency in *where* they position the camera, which makes it hard to compare multiple videos.

For example, if your camera is too far behind your body at address position, it'll make your takeaway look too far inside. This incorrect position will also make it seem like the club is across the line at the top of your backswing.

Conversely, if your camera is too far outside your body, it'll make your takeaway appear too far outside and disconnected, which might make the top of your swing look too flat.

The key is to make sure the tripod is positioned at your mid-torso and directly behind your hands. This will provide the perfect angle to analyze your takeaway, backswing, transition, and downswing.

Angle #2: Face On

With the face-on angle, you can see ball position, grip, stance, weight distribution, impact position, and more. To position correctly, make sure the camera gets your full swing in the frame and the camera is in the middle of your chest.

When you record your swing in the same position each time, it's easy for you or a swing coach to compare side-by-side swings. For extra credit, get some videos in slow motion mode as it's even easier to analyze your swing. Plus, they look 100X cooler too.

Record swing videos from when you're hitting it well and not so well can also help you learn more about your game. This makes it easier to fix things mid-round if you are hitting it poorly as you learn more about your swing. Also, don't forget to record less than full swings such as pitches, chips, bunker shots, and more. The more you can document your game the better.

Remember, progress is sometimes slow in golf and it's easy to feel like you aren't making changes. But when you have an archive of videos to document your swing evolution, it's easy to see your progress.

20. Change Your Range (Practice inside 125 Yards)

◆

As I mentioned initially, most golfers hit far too many mid to long irons in practice. These just aren't shots you will ever hit that consistently even if you're a top-ranked player in the world.

→ **Wicked Smart Fact**

In the 2021 PGA Tour season, the average green in regulation (GIR) percentage was 65.14%. Not only do the best players in the world miss greens with perfect swings, they also don't hit it as close to the pin as you might think. When they hit the green, here is the average proximity to the hole:

- 200-225 yards: 42'
- 175-200 yards: 34'1"
- 150-175 yards: 27'8"
- 125-150 yards: 23'2"

If the best players in the world only hit 65% of greens and don't average inside 25 feet from 150+ yards, there's no need for you to hit ball after ball on the driving range with mid to long irons. It's just a waste of time and not helping you get closer to hitting your golf goals.

If you want to get better and fulfill your golfing potential, spend 70% of your time practicing from short range. *Why 70%* you might wonder?

Because about 70% of all shots in an average round happen inside 125 yards. More importantly, they're easier shots to improve and thus directly impact your ability to shoot lower scores. Meanwhile, refining your irons and drivers is more complex and doesn't always lead to lower scores in the short term.

Yet, if you watch most golfers practice, inside 125 yards is almost ignored. I can't tell you how often I go to the golf course and see the range full of people mindlessly hitting 7 irons or fairway woods and hybrids they use a few times per round (at most).

Meanwhile, no one is just hitting wedges for an entire bucket and the short game area is empty.

This is ironic because nearly every golfer says they want to play more consistently above all else. Don't get me wrong; I understand why so many golfers neglect practice from inside 125 yards. Bombing drivers on the range is more fun than grinding away on the short game area.

But what's the point of being the best driver if you still make bogeys or don't capitalize with good approach shots after you hit a perfect drive?

For me, few things in golf are more frustrating than bombing it 300 yards, hitting an awful wedge shot to 40 feet, or even missing the green. Rather than the opposite, I would rather spray it all over the golf course and scramble with a wicked good short game.

As you plan your practice sessions, emphasize inside 125 yards. It's the fastest way to shoot lower scores *without* changing your swing. Section four will focus more on this to help you become a wedge wizard.

21. Set Up for Success

♦

While I'm a huge proponent of practicing your short game, you obviously still need a dependable full swing. Every player has a different swing and I'm not here to tell you one way vs. another. But after working with world-class instructors like Boyd Summerhays and other great coaches over 25 years of playing golf, I've noticed that they all emphasize one thing—**setup position**.

Your setup is the start of grooving a consistent, repeatable swing and makes your success inevitable.

When you set up the golf ball and target in a neutral position and with perfect alignment to your target, it's much easier to make better contact and hit the ball consistently well. However, if you're set up incorrectly, a lot can go wrong *before* you ever take the club away on your backswing.

Therefore, you see PGA Tour players work on their setup position more than anything else on the range. They know that if their alignment, posture, ball position, grip, or something else is off, their swing won't produce their desired results. As Daniel Coyle said in *The Little Red Book*, *"You might be surprised to learn that many top performers place great importance on practicing the same skills they practice as beginners."*

It's true—there are only so many components to the golf swing. Fundamentals like setup are the key to playing your most consistent golf ever. Regardless of swing changes you're working on at the driving range, always master your setup.

When you're hitting it well, make sure to video your swing so you have a template for a great starting position. If you're in a slump and can't seem to find the center of the face if your life depends on it, check your setup position before changing anything else. Chances are your alignment, ball position, posture, or something simple is off.

Unfortunately, so many golfers tweak everything else *before* first ensuring their address position is correct.

Here's a good example from my own golf career.

In 2019, I struggled with a move that 90% of all golfers struggle with—coming over the top. I would take the club too far inside on the takeaway and get steep on the way down.

The result was a weak pull cut.

While I needed to strengthen my grip, the main reason I was getting too steep was my setup. My feet were right of the target, while my hips and shoulders were well left. Had I shallowed the club on the downswing properly, I would barely have contacted the golf ball because my lines were crossed.

Once my instructor helped me straighten out my lines and improve my address position, it made it so much easier to take the club back square and drop it in the slot. While I had to make other adjustments as well, none would have worked *without* adjusting my setup first.

Here is the real reason setup matters more than you might think.

Even if you don't consciously realize where you're aligned, your subconscious mind is aware. Your mind knows if you're right or left of the target and adjusts throughout your swing to counteract your alignment.

That's why I see so many guys aimed way right (I'm talking 20–40 yards), but they don't realize it. On the backswing, their mind is thinking, *Wow, we are aimed way right ... we better come over the top to get it back left and toward the target*, which leads to manipulating their swing to compensate for poor alignment.

To make matters worse, this overcompensation can work sometimes. You can aim well to the right of your intended target but somehow pull it back and hit it close. This makes you think you made a perfect swing when your aim was off, but your mind was able to fix your error by making an incorrect swing move. Over time, this can lead to some bad habits that are hard to break.

Conversely, the opposite can happen. For example, if you're aimed right of your target and hit it dead straight, you will miss to the right, making you think you pushed the shot when you hit it dead straight. Like the other scenario, this can lead to new swing problems and bad habits that are hard to break.

That's why your setup is so damn important, it will fix so many swing issues and avoid so many down the road. Keep working on your setup position for as long as you play golf!

22. Perfect Your Pre-Shot Routine on the Range

◆

After setup, the second most essential thing you can't practice enough is your pre-shot routine. Like a good starting position, it's one of the few things that all elite players have in common.

As I mentioned initially, if you watch most average golfers on the range they never spend time going through their pre-shot routine. Most rapidly fire one golf ball after another, hoping to somehow magically get better. This leads to rarely having a dependable routine on the golf course either.

A pre-shot routine is something you need to first create and then practice on the range. Don't just hope it shows up on the course for you if you haven't spent time honing it at the practice tee.

Pre-shot routines are part of sports. Just think about NFL kickers before they line up for a field goal or basketball players at the free-throw line. Each player develops their own pre-shot routine to stay focused and feel confident.

Helen Alfredsson described the importance of a pre-shot routine in the book *A Good Swing Is Hard to Find*. She stated, *"A pre-shot routine helps you build a cocoon around yourself. This is the mysterious zone that athletes refer to longingly. But there's nothing mysterious about it."*

A pre-shot routine is one of the few constants in golf and like a lot of the first section, something that you can control. A pre-shot routine will also help you:

- Stay calm and focused
- Improve your pace of play
- Block out negative thoughts
- Find your target and commit to a shot

- Take your range game to the golf course

But most importantly, it will help you get into the zone. When your pre-shot routine becomes automatic, you can easily get in the zone and let your subconscious take over. This is where greatness comes and it's almost an out-of-body experience.

To get these benefits on the golf course, you need to first create your routine on the range.

To give you an example, here, I summarize my pre-shot routine for an approach shot into the green:

- Get to the ball, assess the lie, assess the wind, laser my distance, figure out where to miss (and where not to miss), pick my intended shot shape and desired target.
- Choose a carry number—the distance I want the shot to travel in the air to give my mind a clear objective for the shot.
- Once I know my carry distance, I grab the right club for the job and take one or two rehearsal swings. This is getting my mind ready to execute the shot and is part of the on-course visualization we covered earlier.
- Then I pick two targets standing behind the ball. One target is by the green (a tree, mound, flagstick). The other target, known as an intermediary target directly in front of my ball (about one or two feet ahead of the ball) and in line with my long range target.
- Once I pick my targets, I take a deep breath and walk to the golf ball after exhaling. This is the magic moment and the breath is very important. This is where you start to switch from your conscious, analytical mind to your subconscious mind. Think of it like a handoff to let your more powerful mind take the reins.
- As I address the golf ball, my focus is on getting my club aligned with my intermediary target. I set up to the ball, *then* look up and confirm the long-range target.
- Finally, I take two waggles, another look at the target, then go.

I go through these steps for every single full-swing shot. Well, I try and get it right about 95% of the time, which gives me confidence on any shot.

Just remember, creating a pre-shot routine is one of the few things you can control on the golf course and can have an enormous impact on your game. If you haven't noticed a theme yet, control what you can to shoot lower scores faster than ever.

23. Use the 80/20 Practice Rule

This lesson is simple—**spend 80% of practice on the weakest parts of your game.** The other 20% of the time you can reinforce your strengths.

Golf is difficult because there are so many components and different shots to master. I know players who are great drivers but can't hit a wedge to save their lives and guys who can putt amazingly well once they're on the green, but their long game holds them back from shooting lower scores.

Golf has a way of showing your weaknesses, so there's no point in avoiding them. Otherwise, you will make the same mistakes over and over again and likely hit a plateau when it comes to lowering your handicap.

Therefore, you need to spend more time on the parts of your game that are holding you back. Whether it's your driver, irons, wedges, sand game, putting, or something else, spend 80% of your time improving it.

The best way to do this is to regularly track your stats after each round. This will make it easy to identify which area of your game to focus on and which ones don't need as much work.

If you've never tracked stats before, don't worry. I'll cover all that in one of the upcoming sections of the book and make it very easy to help you identify your weaknesses. When you use the 80/20 rule, your weaknesses will become strengths quickly which will help you shoot lower scores more consistently.

24. Get Better with Technical Practice

No matter how good you get, you'll always have something to work on in this crazy game of golf. When you're working on technical swing changes, using drills or training aids, this is known as **technical practice.**

It's sometimes referred to as block practice as you're working to change a part of your swing for a chunk (aka "block") of time. Maybe it's the transition, takeaway, grip, or something else. Usually, this is done with various drills or training aids to help you *feel* your new swing changes.

The goal with block practice isn't so much to hit each shot at full speed but to make lasting change through repetition. This is one of the few times you need to hit more range balls to retrain your muscles.

To make the most of block practice, follow these rules:

- **Use short-to-mid irons:** Making big swing changes with a driver is much harder than with a mid-to-short iron. A driver has the least loft and is the longest club, which makes it the most difficult one to control. So put the big stick back in the bag (for now) until you feel comfortable with shorter clubs. Then work your way up to longer clubs and finally, your driver.
- **Swing at half speed to feel the change**: Slow it down, put your ego aside, and work on feeling the changes without the ball going 100% of its normal distance. Start with half swings at 50% speed and work your way up. It's a lot easier to feel swing changes when you're at less than full speed.
- **Take regular breaks**: While you will need to hit more balls to feel the change, make sure you're taking breaks regularly. After every five or 10 balls, take a short break, breathe, and take some slow motion practice swings before hitting another range ball.

- **Stay consistent:** Changing your swing is hard work and there will be sessions where it feels like you'll never hit it well again. Stay persistent, trust the process (or your swing coach), and keep grinding. Sometimes you have to dig it out on the range for what feels like forever before seeing real results. As Gary Player said, *"The harder you practice, the luckier you get."*

Finally, don't practice like this all the time. There's a time and place for block practice, drills, and training aids. It is not all the time, though!

I would argue it's not over 20% of your entire driving range sessions either. If you always practice this way, you will never feel comfortable with your golf swing and will be thinking about mechanics on the golf course—which rarely leads to low scores.

25. Use Tiger's 9-Shot Practice Drill

◆

While block practice is good for making swing changes, it doesn't prepare you for the golf course. This is one reason why so many golfers are great on the range but can't seem to take their game to the course. Instead, spend some practice time honing your skills, aka skills practice, so you're ready for the golf course.

One of the best tests of this is Tiger Woods' patented "9 Shot" practice drill. This drill makes you hit different flights and trajectories to make the most of each session.

To get started, grab a 6 or 7 iron. Then try to hit all nine of these shots:

- Low trajectory - straight ball flight, cut, and draw.
- High trajectory - straight ball flight, cut, and draw.
- Normal trajectory - straight ball flight, cut, and draw.

Try it with nine balls first and see how many you can hit. Then try again, and hopefully, one day soon, you can reach all nine shots in a row. Use your driver instead of a mid-iron to make it an even more challenging practice session.

If you can hit all nine shots with any club in the bag, you will become unstoppable on the golf course. This is a simple, fun way to practice any day of the week. The 9-ball drill instantly shows you if you need to work on the trajectory of ball flight and prepares you for any shot you might face during a round.

26. Mix It Up (Random Practice)

◆

Block practice is necessary occasionally as is skills practice. But sometimes, you need to mix it up even more to simulate golf on the course. Random practice is simple—never hit the same shot twice. Keep your mind guessing by changing up clubs, targets, and the goal for each shot.

Think about it; how often do we hit 7-iron after 7-iron on the driving range… When's the last time you did that on the golf course? Unless you hit an iron into a hazard or out of bounds, my guess is rarely.

If you're feeling lost (or forget to plan before your session), **try out random practice after warming up**.

Make it a goal not to hit the same shot twice or even use the same club twice. This is your time to get creative and become an artist on the golf course. Hit shots that challenge you, hit your favorite shots, hard shots, and ones you don't normally face. Hit some high, then low, then left, then right, and remember to take breaks to simulate breaks between shots on the golf course.

Doing this will make you pick a new target, go through your routine, and keep your mind guessing. Plus, it's a lot more fun than doing drills or using training aids all the time.

27. Two Types of Speed Sessions

Distance is a highly debated topic in today's world of golf, but I'm here to say increasing your distance makes golf easier. In high school, my driver didn't even go 200 yards, and now I carry it 280 or more yards. Trust me when I say that playing with wedges and short irons makes golf a lot easier to score low and consistently well.

Even if you aren't always straight down the middle, I would rather have a wedge from the rough than a 7 iron from the fairway.

The key to more distance is speed; which is why speed training has become a popular trend. With consistent training, it can have an incredible effect on your game. Plus, you can speed train on or off the golf course.

Here are my two favorite methods to speed train:

SuperSpeed Sticks

These weighted sticks have revolutionized speed training and are used by amateurs and professionals worldwide. These weighted sticks make it easy to learn how to swing faster and more efficiently by training your muscles. Follow the protocol on their website and stay consistent to get awesome results. From juniors to seniors, there is a set for everyone.

To learn more about this training aid, visit the bonus section at www.wickedsmartgolf.com/book

Speed Sessions

No worries if you don't want to invest in the SuperSpeed sticks; you can still speed train to gain distance. The other speed training you can do is a *"speed session."*

Sometimes I dedicate part or all of my driving range time to only focusing on speed. After warming up (please always warm-up before speed training), I focus on speed above all else. I don't care where the ball goes and instead swing as hard as I can.

Like the SuperSpeed sticks, this will train your body and muscles to get comfortable with higher speeds. Try to limit these to once or twice a week (at most) and never before playing a round of golf. I've found doing a full-speed training session on the day of a round can zap your energy and throw off your timing.

With enough time, this will increase your swing speed, which will increase your distance. To make the most of these sessions, I highly recommend investing in a launch monitor or other device to track your swing speed progress over time.

28. Get Back to Basics

♦

No matter how good you get in golf, never forget the importance of mastering the basics. Make it a point to only focus on the big three during certain practice sessions.

As Jim Flick said in *On Golf*, *"The high handicapper can knock five to ten strokes off their game in a month just by working conscientiously on three things; posture, grip pressure, and alignment."*

I would argue this is true for all levels of golfers. While a single-digit handicap might not drop as many shots, focusing on the fundamentals is never bad.

While we covered alignment in-depth in a previous lesson, don't forget about posture and grip pressure. Both play a vital role in improving your ball striking and are easy to work on in practice.

- **Posture**: Like alignment, if your posture is off, it can alter your swing without you realizing it. That's why it's so important to regularly record and analyze your swing to double-check your posture. Evaluate your knee flex, the tilt of your spine, and how close you're standing to the golf ball.
- **Grip pressure**: Don't forget to check your grip pressure too. This is harder to monitor, since you can't spot it when recording your swing, but also very significant as too much grip pressure leads to excess tension in your swing. However, not gripping the club firmly enough can affect your path and clubhead at impact.

These two fundamentals, with great alignment, will help you tremendously. Set time in your practice schedule every week or month to go back to the basics.

29. Dial in Your Distances

◆

To play wicked smart golf, you need to know your carry distances for each club.

If you don't know how far each club goes, you're making golf harder on yourself. It's too easy nowadays with launch monitors and free golf GPS apps not to know your distance with each club in the bag.

On the driving range, get clear about how far each club travels in the air.

It's not a perfect science with range balls, mats, etc., but do your best to have a number for each club. This is assuming you hit it at 100% effort, not a knockdown type of shot. Over a few range sessions, hit 20-25 golf balls with each club, log the distances in your phone, remove any bad swings, and average out your distance.

Things change with cold/warm weather, wind, elevation, and other factors, but you should have a baseline for each club. This will help you speed up play, pull each club out with confidence, and ultimately shoot lower scores. Once you know your numbers, write them in a note on your phone or a notecard that you keep in your golf bag as a constant reminder. When you get new clubs, update your distances too.

30. Play a Round on the Range

◆

Another great practice routine is to play a round on the range. After a quick warm-up, play 9 or 18 holes *without* leaving the practice tee. This is a great way to enhance your imagination and mix up your practice routine.

For example, imagine a course you often play (or the one you're practicing at) and the first tee shot. Create an imaginary fairway between two targets on the driving range, go through your pre-shot routine, and hit the shot as if you're on the first tee.

Then play the next shot from where your drive would end up as if you were on the golf course. Do this for 9 or 18 holes to enhance your practice session and simulate a real round of golf. If there is a putting green nearby, you can even go back and forth from the driving range to simulate scrambling and putting.

Aside from helping your imagination, this is also a great way to hone your pre-shot routine. Just make sure not to rapid-fire through each hole and instead slow down as if you were on the golf course.

The more realistic you make this simulation during practice, the more comfortable you will feel on the golf course. This is another great way to effectively take your driving range to the golf course.

31. Practice Where You Play

Let's face it, sometimes hitting golf ball after golf ball on the driving range gets old. Occasionally you need to take your skills and test them in real situations on the golf course. If you can find a time when the tee sheet isn't booked, play a round but in practice mode on the course.

As Tom Doak said in *Anatomy of a Golf Course*, "*The only truly perfect practice facility is an empty golf course. Because only there is it possible to practice every stroke one might need to get the ball in the hole.*"

On-course practice is a great way to hit shots you can't hit at the practice facility. I always suggest finding shots that scare you and hitting them as well.

For example, if you hate a certain tee shot at your local course, drop a few balls and hit it a few times. Try the tee shot with a few different clubs and trajectories until you get comfortable with it. Tackle these fears head-on in practice, so you're no longer scared of them during a normal round of golf.

Other shots you can't practice at most facilities but can on the golf course include:

- Fairway bunkers
- Pitches over water
- Thick lies in the rough
- Chips/pitches from deep rough
- Long bunker shots (20–40 yards)
- Bump 'n' run shots with a tier on the green
- Long putts with a steep uphill/downhill slope

Or any shot you want to work on but can't at your normal practice facility.

Other ways to have fun with on-course practice include:

- **Worst ball scramble**: Play two balls on each hole and keep selecting the worst of the two until the hole is done. See how low your worst ball score can get. Golf might feel a lot easier when you get to play your best ball.
- **Only hit odd or even clubs**: Challenge yourself by only hitting odd or even clubs on certain days. This will help you become more creative and learn how to hit different trajectories, shot shapes, and become an artist on the golf course.
- **Never hit driver**: Instead of bombing drivers all day, only hit fairway woods or hybrids off the tee. This will test your long game and find any weaknesses or awkward distances you need to improve.
- **Play a variety of tee boxes**: Instead of playing the same set of tees you normally play, mix it up. Play a different box on each hole to change your distances and hit different clubs than normal.

32. Tee It Forward to Go Low

If you're like most golfers, you always want to shoot your lowest score ever. Maybe it's breaking 90, 80, 70, or even eclipsing par.

While you might have the ability to shoot those numbers, sometimes the mental side of things might hold you back. Often we get in our heads when trying to shoot a new low number. I hope the tips in section one will help you master your mind, but there is another way I've used to get comfortable shooting lower scores.

While on-course practice is a super effective way to improve your game, another way is to tee it forward. Sometimes playing up a tee box from normal is a great way to get comfortable going low and breaking through plateaus. Not to mention, help you become a better wedge player as you will shorter approach shots into the green.

After playing in a monthhly two-man scramble tournament with my buddy Jacob, I realized the importance of mixing up tee boxes. We consistently finish in the top five and have epic days of eight birdies in a row and shooting in the 50s to get the win.

Sure, we fired low rounds because it was a scramble, but we also don't play the tips like normal. After playing up one tee box and making the course about 400 yards shorter, it made us both get comfortable going low. It made it easier to attack pins and drain more putts under pressure. When I found myself in a normal tournament weeks and months later, I had the same "attack" mentality.

For example, if you've never broken 80 and always play the same tees, go up a box. I've found that often it's in our head more than anything else. You should be able to break 80 quickly and can get the monkey off your back. Not only do you finally score in the 70s, but it will feel more normal to your mind. Soon enough, you will be comfortable going low and can do it from your normal tee box too.

33. Improve Your Physical Conditioning

I've outlined a ton of ways to practice on the range and course to get better, but I can't forget about fitness either. Changing your physique can have an enormous effect on your golf game.

Let's face it; the golf swing is difficult on the body. Consistently turning at high speeds, in one direction, repeatedly isn't natural. After enough rounds of golf and endless buckets of balls, it can lead to many imbalances in your body. Therefore, you need to stay ahead of potential injuries, so you're not sidelined while your buddies are out golfing.

Aside from injury, the stronger you are, the easier it is to hit it longer too. Don't get me wrong; distance isn't everything, but it makes the game easier. Plus, data from the PGA Tour using ShotLink technology shows the shorter distance on your approach shots, the closer your proximity to the hole.

I like to think about golf and fitness in two categories; *training and recovery*. Each plays a pivotal role in helping you shoot your best scores.

First is training with cardio, weight training, and other exercises like swimming. While I'm not saying you need to turn into the Hulk-like Bryson DeChambeau to hit it 300+ yards, improving your fitness can help your golf game. Plus, regular exercise can help with your overall health, improve your mindset, and have tons of other positive effects.

Second, recovery is very important, especially if you exercise and play golf regularly. It's critical to get your body back to normal from the stress of golf and exercise. Some of my favorite recover methods are foam rolling, stretching, massages, chiropractic work, acupuncture, yoga, and more. As Jim Rohn said, *"Take care of your body. It's the only place you have to live."*

Stick to something you can do regularly and incorporate it as part of your routine. Then add plenty of recovery to avoid injuries and play this game for as long as physically possible.

34. Practice Less to Get Better

Sometimes the best practice is no practice at all. I know it's hard to think about, but too much time on the range can hurt your game. Too much practice can also lead to setting unrealistic expectations about your game.

Here's an example…

When I joined a country club in 2018 to pursue professional golf, I felt like I had to practice daily for two reasons. First, I wanted to get my money's worth and second, I thought daily practice was the only way to improve.

Some sessions were great and left me feeling like I would never shoot over par. Other sessions were so bad I debated ever swinging a club again. Sometimes, I would get worse from overdoing it and burning myself out instead of getting better. Plus, I kind of dreaded going to the golf course to practice. Obviously, I don't want that for you as golf is supposed to be fun.

If you're feeling more dread than excitement when you head to the course, take a short break from the game. Don't worry; your swing won't magically disappear either.

Often, when you take a small break from golf, you come back with a better attitude and much fewer swing thoughts. This clean slate makes it fun and refreshing to get back on the course.

If you practice 24/7, it's also easy to overanalyze your game and get into "playing the golf swing" vs. "playing golf." As you'll learn in the next section, there is a huge difference! This is another reason so many players are great on the driving range but can't seem to take their game to the course.

If you're feeling burnt out, take some time away from the game. I promise you will return more motivated than ever and appreciate it even more than you thought possible.

Bonus Video

Don't forget to watch the bonus materials at www.wickedsmartgolf.com/book to recap the most efficient ways to practice like a professional. Plus, you can join my free video series to go on the range with me to make each session more effective than ever.

Section III: Peaceful Putting

Discover how to find inner peace on the greens so you can make more putts than ever before

Putting is one of the most important parts of golf and often the least understood. It's also the least practiced and feels like torture for most players... which is why most players skip regular practice.

Yet roughly 40% or more of all shots happen on the green or fringe. If you aren't wildly confident with your flat stick, golf is much more difficult. Just look at what some of the greatest players ever have said about putting:

- *"Half of golf is fun; the other half is putting."* - Peter Dobereiner
- *"Putting is a fascinating, aggravating, wonderful, terrible, and almost incomprehensible part of the game of golf."* - Arnold Palmer
- *"There is no similarity between golf and putting; they are two different games, one played in the air, and the other on the ground."* - Ben Hogan
- *"Putting is two percent technique. Ninety-eight percent desire and determination."* — Jack Nicklaus

Putting is such a critical part of the game that Earl Woods taught Tiger how to play golf from the green, back to the tee. Clearly, it worked because Tiger arguably has the best hands in golf and is the best clutch putter of all time. If my life depended on a putt, he's the guy I would trust to make it. But the main reason I dedicate an entire pillar for putting is…

Improving your putting is the easiest way to drop shots. Getting better on the greens is so much easier than creating a textbook golf swing.

Yet, even though we all know the saying, *"Drive for show, putt for dough,"* most golfers don't practice putting enough (or at all). Just visit your local golf course or driving range and you'll see 90% of players on the range, maybe 10% on the putting green. For the 10% who are on the putting green, most players just use it to feel out the speed before teeing off, instead of building a repeatable stroke and routine.

While putting practice is important, it's *how* you practice that matters. Like your full swing, it's not how long you're on the practice green. More practice doesn't mean you will become a better putter. Instead, the goal for each session is to build your confidence, which, as you will learn, isn't about spending countless hours on the putting green.

My goal for you by the end of this section is to have clarity about what you need to do to improve your putting. My aim is for you to feel at peace on the greens and trust your stroke not frantically worry as you stand over every putt. I want you to have Tiger-like confidence on the greens so you can play your best golf.

Before diving into my best-putting strategies to become a wicked smart golfer, I think it's important to see the PGA Tour averages for certain length putts. Because if you're like most golfers, you're likely under the assumption that the best players in the world make every putt they attempt. This isn't true, when in reality you're just seeing the highlight reel that will keep people from not skipping channels.

→ **Wicked Smart Fact: PGA Tour Putting Averages - 2021 Season**

- 3 feet: 99.46%
- 4 feet: 92.19%
- 5 feet: 81.49%
- 6 feet: 70.34%
- 7 feet: 61.64%
- 8 feet: 52.94%
- 9 feet: 46.58%
- 10 feet: 42.24%
- 10-15 feet: 30%
- 15-20 feet: 18%
- 20-25 feet: 12%
- Over 25 feet: 5%

The first takeaway is that you need to master your 3-5 footers. It's one of the easiest ways to shave strokes from your scorecard and 10X easier than learning how to change your swing.

When doing the research, the statistics that surprised me were the 6-10 footers. PGA players rarely make much outside of 20 feet consistently, so don't beat yourself up so much. Instead, use these stats to reset your expectations and not try to force everything in and let it happen.

Plus, if the best players in the world who have unlimited time to practice don't make more than half of their putts past nine feet, no amount of time on the green will help you from that range. You're simply not going to beat the pros. Use your practice time to refine your stroke and putting routine to become automatic from short range.

Here are the most effective tips to help you find peace when pulling the putter out of the bag.

35. Play the Right Putter

◆

There is no doubt in my mind that your putter is the most important club in your bag. Before sharing the best putting tips and ways to practice, you need to have the right putter for your stroke.

You need to love your putter like a dear friend or family member; it should be your favorite club in the bag.

Even if it costs more than your driver, it's worth every penny and will last for years or decades. It's funny because so many golfers aren't afraid to spend $500 on a custom-fit driver. But for buying a putter, they get cheap, don't go through a proper fitting, and settle for something off the rack.

When you look down at your putter, you want to think about one thing: **confidence**. Your putter should give you borderline insane amounts of swagger on the greens. You should have so much confidence that it's borderline cocky (but don't go too much or you will anger the Golf Gods). Hopefully, you get the point, though; your putter should feel like a security blanket.

I'm not here to tell you which brand or type to buy because every player is different. Here are

three things you should think about when picking out your putter:

1. **Putter style**: First, you need to pick the right putter style to match your stroke. The three options are *blade, mallet, and high* MOI. A blade putter is the oldest in golf and best for an in to out stroke. A mallet putter is best if you take the putter straight back and straight through. A high MOI (like a TaylorMade Spider) works for either. The high MOI is the newest and most forgiving type putter loved by PGA Tour pros and all levels of amateur golfers.
2. **Putter length**: Once you find the right style, find the right length putter too. I've found that most players use a putter too long for them,

which doesn't allow them to set up to the ball properly. Test out different lengths to find what suits your posture and height best.
3. **Putter grip**: Finally, don't forget your grip. You want your putter grip to match how you hold the putter (traditional, cross-handed, claw, etc.). And should regrip regularly so you don't let a worn down grip affect your putting.

Finding the right putter for you is step one to becoming a confident putter.

36. Become "Automatic" on the Greens

◆

In the mental game section, I elaborated on the subconscious vs. conscious mind to play your best golf. The more you understand how they both work, the easier it is to play your best golf.

With putting, your subconscious mind needs to be the one that's in control of your stroke.

Why?

Because putting is all about feel, imagination, and trust. It's not about mechanics nearly as much as most golfers think.

Using my subconscious mind helped me drop four strokes from my game in less than 12 months. I went from averaging close to 34 putts per round to about 29 putts per round from the 2020–2021 season. The best part was that I was practicing substantially less than before.

To get these crazy results, I didn't change my putter, my stroke, or anything else. All that changed was my routine. I learned how to play *"Automatic Golf"* by tapping into the power of my subconscious mind.

How?

By learning to keep my conscious busy with a secondary task as I go from behind the golf ball to standing over it. As I walk toward the ball, I begin counting down from 100 in my head. My routine takes about six seconds and I take the putter back when I'm at 94.

It sounds ridiculously simple, I know; but hear me out. Here's what the creator, Cameron Strachan, said about the *"Look and Shoot"* method:

"When you're counting you can't be worried about your score, the line or anything else that golfers like to think about. This is because we can only think of one thought at a time."

Since I am counting, I no longer think about the putt anymore. I don't have any other thoughts because my conscious mind was busy counting down from 100. This is important because the conscious mind can't have more than one thought at a time. For example, if you're feeling anxious, change your thinking to something you're grateful for. When you are feeling grateful, it's impossible to be anxious as well.

With putting, while my conscious mind is busy, I trust my subconscious mind to feel the speed of the putt. Don't get me wrong; I still read greens mainly to supply this information to my mind and paint a clear picture of the hole — that all happens behind the hole. But, once I cross an imaginary line and I'm over the ball, I'm *not* thinking about anything else other than counting down, I'm relying on my subconscious (the much more powerful part of the mind) to do the job for me.

As Cameron and I discussed in a podcast interview, you can become a good putter if you can throw a baseball. When you throw a baseball, you don't think about mechanics—you aren't thinking, "I just need to grip the baseball tight, load my arm up, accelerate on the follow-through, and turn my body." Instead, you see a mitt and throw the baseball at it. There is no conscious effort once you learn how to throw a baseball.

The same goes for putting. Yet, most of us overcomplicate putting when it's no different from throwing a baseball. Once you learn how to putt, you can do it automatically.

Things go wrong on the putting green when you try to control everything. When your conscious mind is overly active, that's when you try to guide putts and look more like a robot than an artist. You want to think of yourself as someone at peace, who simply looks at the putt, then makes it happen.

This is why kids are such good putters; they see the hole and putt to it. They keep things simple and don't get bogged down in all the mechanics as adults do. By putting with freedom, they can tap into their subconscious and simply let go.

While practice is important to an extent, it's not everything with putting. Cameron Strachan had to say this about how most people practice putting incorrectly:

"Spending vast amounts of time practicing your putting is a waste of valuable time. It's simply not necessary. When you have learned to perform your own natural putting game subconsciously, you are stuck with it. It is not going to go away, even if you don't practice. You never forget how to ride a bike or drive a car - so don't bother with long practice sessions, you have better things to do."

The concept is simple, but by far the most effective I've ever used in 20+ years of playing golf. It truly changed my putting and I am glad I learned about this simple system sooner rather than later.

To become a great putter, quit making things so complicated. See the hole, give it a quick read, and putt to it. Remember, if you can throw a baseball, you can become a good putter.

🎙 PODCAST Episode:

To learn more about the Look and Shoot method to become automatic on the green, make sure to listen to the Wicked Smart Golf Podcast episodes.
Visit www.wickedsmartgolf.com/book to listen now.

37. Prepare Your Mind for the Putt

♦

As I mentioned in the mental game pillar, I worked with a sports psychologist before going to Q-School in 2019. One of the biggest things I wanted to discuss with him was putting, as I knew I had serious room to improve. I remember telling him, *"Sometimes I kind of blank on the greens and forget what I'm doing. I lose focus and kind of space out."*

His solution was to give my mind a clear breakdown of the putt. He told me from behind the ball, read the putt, analyze the green's slope, and then declare it to your mind. It worked wonders at Q-School and still something I do with every putt to this day.

Now, after reading the putt, I give my mind a clear image of how the putt should break. I will say to myself (in my head), *Okay, I got ten feet, uphill, right to left. My aim is just outside the right part of the cup.*

This gives my mind a clear image of what the putt should do and helps clarify the goal. It also forces me to pick a line so I can hit the putt with conviction.

The more specific the description, the better. As Billy Casper said, *"Try to think where you want to put the ball, not where you don't want it to go."* To give yourself a clear picture of the putt, you need to use a few green-reading techniques that I'll discuss in the next point.

38. Simplify Green Reading

Green reading is an art but one you can learn over time. I'm proof you can improve your green reading because one thing I forgot to mention is that I have only one eye. Well, I mean, I have both eyes, but the right one doesn't work so well (about 20/400 vision). If I close my left eye, all I see is blurry shapes, which obviously isn't ideal for reading greens. No surgeries or procedures can work, so I've learned to deal with it.

Like putting in general, I think most people overcomplicate green reading as well. After working with tons of different coaches and reading endless golf books, I like to keep things simple.

Here are my green-reading rules to help you simplify the process.

1. **Trust your gut.** Your first instinct is almost always right for reading greens. I think 90% or more of the time, what you initially see is how the putt will break. I like to think this is your subconscious at work. You want to trust it often. While it's not perfect, no green-reading method is, so go with your gut.
2. **Only read the putt from behind the hole.** For most golfers, only read the putt from behind the golf ball. Reading the putt from behind the hole *and* behind the putt slows down play and can easily confuse you. Only resort to reading from both sides if you aren't sure of the break, it's a long putt, it has multiple tiers or is a double breaker.
3. **Factor in grain.** Depending on where you play, grain will affect the break of the putt. As Raymond Floyd said in the *Elements of Scoring*, "*A putt traveling in the grain will roll slower and not as far. When the grain is running across on a level putt, the ball will break in the direction of the grain. Grain tends to grow along the direction of a slope, or the way the water runs off the green.*"
4. **Don't get too caught up with how much the putt will break.** Some players stress themselves out on the exact break, but it rarely does any good. Research has found the best players in the world can't do this successfully, so don't put too much pressure on yourself.

Instead, focus on the start line (the first 18 inches) more than anything else.

5. **Add more break to mid-long-range putts.** In an interview, Phil Mickelson said that when he plays with amateurs in pro-am events, the biggest thing he notices is that most players under-read putts. When a putt is under-read, you have a small chance of the ball going in the hole. You must get lucky and hope that it catches an edge. Meanwhile, over-reading a putt gives you a much better chance of draining the putt.

6. **Commit to a line.** There's nothing worse than standing over a putt feeling indecisive about the break or speed. Before starting your pre-shot putting routine, decide on the break and apex. I've found that when you aren't sure and are second-guessing yourself, it's easy to hit the putt too soft and try to guide it into the hole. This rarely turns out well and usually ends up short with zero chance of finding the bottom of the cup. Get clear in your mind, so you hit the putt with conviction.

39. Line Up Putts

Once you have read the green and found your start line, use your golf ball to help you to aim properly. You can draw a line on the ball or use the side logo arrows to aim the putt at your intended start line. This gives you a clear visual and makes it easy to line your putter up with the line to set up square to the target.

So many golfers skip this step, then have no clue where they were supposed to aim when they're standing over the ball. This is too simple to not do every single time and one of the common things that nearly every professional golfer does on every putt.

Once your ball is aimed at the start line, use the alignment aid on your putter to match the line on your golf ball. This should lead you to feeling very confident over any putt on the green and help the ball start on line properly.

Remember, putting is more about confidence than anything else!

If you're standing over the putt with any doubt about your line or arrows being incorrect, step back, reset your golf ball, and then go through your routine again. Don't waste shots from being indecisive over putts when alignment is something in your control.

40. Keep Your Head Down

◆

Never forget, putting is all about getting the ball in the hole — it's *not* about perfect mechanics.

Form and technique aren't nearly as important with putting as they are with the full swing. For example, Jack Nicklaus had a very different stroke than Tiger Woods or Arnold Palmer. But all these golf legends got the ball in the hole with their unique stroke and style.

However, they and all good putters have one thing in common — **they keep their head down and don't peak too early.** They make sure the ball is well off the putter face *before* looking up to watch the putt.

Normally I think "Keep your head down" is the worst golf advice ever. Except with putting, because when you look up too early, you change the path and plane of the stroke. It's easy to miss putts off-line and leave them short because you aren't making as good contact when you peek too early.

For short putts especially, try to *hear* the ball hit the bottom of the cup, not see it. This will train you to keep your head down long enough not to let excess movement affect your putting stroke.

41. Get the Ball to the Hole

There is a ZERO percent chance of a putt that is short of going in the hole. Sure, your friends will call you "Alice" and a lot of other things, but the worst part is knowing the putt had no chance of going in.

The perfect missed putt is 18 inches past the hole.

It's still a tap in and you know that you at least gave it a chance to fall into the bottom of the cup, even if you didn't read the green quite right.

Here are three reasons most players leave putts short.

1. **Deceleration**. This is when you take a longer back stroke than forward stroke and it happens a lot with short putts. To eliminate the deceleration, use something I learned from Phil Mickelson for short putts. He calls it the 25/75 rule. If your entire stroke is 100%, make your backstroke 25% and the forward 75%. This ensures you accelerate through the putt and get the ball to the hole. If you feel like you're stabbing at putts with this ratio, change it to 35:65%. Remember, you need to accelerate on every putt, regardless of length.
2. **Pressure**. Under pressure, it's common to leave putts short and hit full shots long, thanks to adrenaline. When you find the butterflies flying around in your stomach, take a deep breath and remind yourself to get the ball to the hole.
3. **Setup issues**. Finally, if you leave putt shorts and it's not caused by decelerating or pressure, it might be your ball position. Often players put the ball too far up or back in their stance. This will cause the putter to either hit down on it or up on it incorrectly. Either way, the ball comes off the face skipping instead of rolling smoothly. When the ball gets airborne and jumps off the face, it loses momentum and ends up short.

Avoiding these three mistakes should help you get the ball to the hole and drain more putts. Plus, when you miss long you already know how the next putt will break.

42. Practice Short Putts Frequently

♦

When you do practice putting, spend the greatest time on the short putts. Dr. Bob Rotella said in *Putting Out of Your Mind* about how professionals practice putting:

"Practicing from close range assures them of making most putts they try. There's nothing better for your confidence and your putting than seeing balls go in the hole time after time."

Aside from confidence, which we all need on the greens, professionals know the critical importance of short putts. Dr. Bob Rotella elaborated by saying,

"If you're solid from, say, two to five feet, it makes it so much easier to make your longer putts. You can stroke them more confidently when you know that if by some misfortune you do miss, you're a cinch to sink the next one."

Short putts are crucial because they are usually to make a birdie or save par after missing the green. The better you feel about your short putts, the easier it is to hit your long putts with a free-flowing stroke.

Plus, mastering short putts is one of the easiest things you can do today, leading to lower scores on the golf course almost instantly. If you must practice putting, practice the short ones to yield the best results for your game.

Bonus Putting Tip: If you find yourself playing fast greens and seem to race each putt by the hole, choke up one inch on the grip. By choking up, you make the putter shorter and it seems to make it easier to make a smaller stroke and get your speed under control.

43. Putt Whenever Possible

◆

When you miss the green, follow this rule: ***If you can putt it, putt it. If you can't putt it, chip it. If you can't chip it, pitch it.***

One of most golfers' biggest mistakes is chipping or pitching instead of putting from off the green. Golf is all about the odds and playing the percentages to manage your way to lower scores.

You are much more likely to hit it closer to the hole with a putter than with a wedge. Sure, it's not as sexy to putt from off the green as it is a high pitch, but it's the higher percentage play. Keep the ball on the ground (or lower to the ground), so once it hits the green, it rolls like a putt.

When you're off the green and choose to putt, you don't need to make many changes either. The only thing you have to worry about is the amount of fringe between you and the green. If it's thicker fringe, you will need to hit it harder. If it's thin and mowed tight, you can putt it nearly the exact same as you would if it was on the green.

44. Putt with a Fairway Wood or Hybrid

As I mentioned in the last tip, you want to putt the golf ball whenever possible from around the green. Even if you're a single-digit handicap, putting is usually the highest percentage shot and will keep the momentum alive during your round.

But if you're off the green and want to putt and there is an obstacle in your way, use a hybrid or 3-wood instead. The ball will pop off the face and then roll out just like a putt once it's on the green. This works great if you have a patch of dead grass in your way or your ball is up against the rough when you're on the fringe.

Here's how to play this shot:

- Grip the club like a putter and choke up all the way to the shaft to shorten the club.
- Address the ball with a narrow stance and 70% of your weight on your left foot (this will make sure you hit down on it). Move the handle up, so you're standing closer to the ball, just like you would with a putter.
- Finally, go through your normal putting routine as if you had a putter in your hand.
- Take your normal putting stroke and trust it.

This is a very useful shot to have around the greens and great for a golf course with a lot of grain. Instead of getting a wedge stuck in the ground, a hybrid or wood will glide right through it and it will roll just like a putt.

Always practice this *before* trying it out on the course. I think you'll find this shot is easier than you think and will save you a ton of strokes by keeping the ball lower and improve your chipping proximity.

45. Invest in an Indoor Putting Green

◆

There is no excuse to not become a good putter, thanks to indoor putting greens. To improve your short game, invest in an indoor putting green. It need not be huge or expensive to help you find peace with the putter.

Remember, most of your time should be spent practicing short putts, not long ones. Remember, even the best players in the world don't make a ton of putts outside 10 feet. Instead, practice the ones that matter most, even if you can only work on your putting indoors.

An indoor mat right by your TV or in your home office is a great way to get extra reps in. Even if you can't make it to the golf course as much as possible, you can hone your putting routine and 10X your confidence with short putts.

I'd argue it's the cheapest yet greatest investment you can make (other than this book, of course). But for your indoor mat to work, you need to put in the reps! Set a daily or weekly goal and leave it somewhere where you're constantly reminded to use it. Make sure to check out the bonuses to learn more about my favorite indoor putting greens at www.wickedsmartgolf.com/book

46. Quit Trying to Lag it Close

I hate it when I'm on the green and hear another player say, *"I'm just trying to lag it close."*

That's a losing mentality. As Dr. Bob Rotella said in *Putting Out of Your Mind*, *"The truth is that every putt is a green light putt."*

So many golfers try not to 3-putt, which leads to a robotic, scared putting stroke that you're trying to control, which usually leads to the thing you didn't want in the first place, a three-putt.

Instead, putt each stroke with confidence and think that it will go in—no matter the length or amount of break.

Of course, not every putt will go in (most won't, in fact), but you must believe that they can drop. You have to play to win instead of trying not to lose (aka, three putting).

When you do have long putts and want to evaluate your putting after the round, think about the 10% rule. For example, if you have a 60-foot putt, anything inside six feet is a win. If you're 40 feet out, get it inside four feet. Don't get me wrong; you're still trying to make it, but the odds are very much against you from this distance.

Always plan to make every putt, but if you're inside 10%, take it and drain the next one.

47. Record Your Putting Stroke

♦

If you're like most golfers, you probably have hundreds of videos of your golf swing but few (if any) of your putting stroke.

To become a master on the greens, you need to know your stroke as well as you know your full swing. Record your putting stroke often so you have a library of putting videos. This will make it so much easier to get out of a slump on the greens and look back to when you were putting great.

One day, I had a terrible putting performance on the green and left everything short. After the round, I had my friend capture my putting stroke in slow-motion and saw the ball was hopping off the face instead of rolling smoothly.

I adjusted my ball position, so I wasn't hitting up on it and instantly fixed my stroke. The next day, I couldn't miss—all from one slow-motion video.

Here are three things to consider when recording your putting stroke.

1. **Record Down the Line**: The first angle you want to capture is down the line. This will make it easy to see if your eye position is over the ball and your path. Plus, you can get a good look at your posture.
2. **Face on Angle**: The second position is to record your stroke face on. This angle will help you see your ball position, arms, grip, and acceleration through the ball.
3. **Slow Motion**: Finally, use your phone to capture slow-motion videos of your putting stroke as well. This will help capture small intricacies you can't get in full-speed recordings like I did when the ball was bouncing too much.

These videos, paired with the tips in lesson #49 will make it easy for you to have tons of confidence on the greens.

48. The Best Training Aid for Putting

◆

You will find hundreds of training aids for your putter if you go on Amazon. But there is only one I use and highly recommend: **the Putting Tutor by Dave Pelz**. Phil Mickelson and his short game coach, Dave Pelz, created this device, so you know it's high quality.

The Putting Tutor is so helpful because it ensures that your start line is correct. If you get the ball started on the incorrect line, you will get instant feedback on whether you're pulling or pushing putts. You can also change the settings to make it more advanced too. The better you get with this device, the easier it will be to shoot lower scores.

The Putting Tutor is simple to use, budget-friendly, and wildly effective. You can use it on an indoor putting green in your home or office or at the golf course. Plus, it's small enough to carry in your bag without taking up space. This is a small investment that I can't recommend enough for all skill levels.

49. How to Give Yourself a Putting Lesson

◆

If you're in a slump, sometimes you need to give yourself a putting lesson.

First, record your stroke using both angles and see if anything sticks out in the videos. Unlike a full swing, it's much easier to analyze your own putting stroke. Since there aren't nearly as many moving parts, it's easier to spot what's going on and fix it quickly.

When reviewing my putting videos, here are questions I like to ask myself:

- *How does my path look?*
- *Is my head coming up too soon?*
- *Are my wrists moving too much?*
- *Do I have the correct ball position?*
- *How is my feet and shoulder alignment?*
- *Are my eyes over or slightly underneath the golf ball?*

Then use the Putting Tutor from the previous lesson to ensure your start line is correct. I love this training aid because it gives instant feedback on whether the ball is starting on the right line.

If all is going well with the Putting Tutor, I suggest using training golf balls. These practice golf balls have a design that makes it easy to see how your ball is rolling. You can easily spot if you're cutting across the ball or shutting the face at impact.

Finally, document your misses after a round if you're in a slump. For example, if you're always missing left, it might be your alignment or your stroke. By summarizing your putting performance, it's easy to spot trends and correct them so you can get out of your funk.

Bonus Video

Don't forget to watch the bonus materials at www.wickedsmartgolf.com/book to recap this section and get more putting tips and tricks.

Section IV: Becoming a Wedge Wizard

Build a solid short game that helps you take advantage of the scoring zone

Hopefully, you're recognizing a theme in this book. Change the smaller things (like mental game, more efficient practice, and putting) *instead* of spending all your time trying to chase the perfect swing on the driving range.

Improving in this area and becoming a wedge wizard is the fastest way to lower your handicap *without* changing your swing. I like to think of this as the scoring zone because everything changes when you improve your short game.

When you have a solid short game, every round gets easier and it actually frees up the rest of your game. Because when things are going well, your short game can turn a good round to a great one. If things aren't going well, your short game can disguise a bad ball striking round and make it easier to drain par putts if you chip it closer.

A good short game will help you keep momentum alive. It's often the par saves that keep your round alive more so than birdies or eagles. It's missing a green or having to chip out from under the trees and making an epic par that keeps the momentum going.

The other secret reason why the short game is so important is because it's an area of the game that's easier to improve. It's a lot easier to learn how to hit a basic chip shot or bunker shot than it is to make a full swing as there are less moving parts. Not to mention, less speed. Plus, this part of the game rarely vanishes like the full swing, once you get the basics it will stick with you and doesn't need total overhauls like the full swing.

Yet, most golfers spend most of their practice outside the scoring zone. Most players prefer to hit drivers and mid-irons in practice *instead* of working on the distance that actually matters.

If you want to become a better golfer, spend most of your practice time inside 125 yards. As Paul Runyan said in *The Short Way to Lower Scoring*, *"Within every golfer there is a vast, untapped potential for improving his short game."*

This section will make it easy to become a wedge wizard and get the most out of your game every time you tee it up.

50. Carry the Right Wedges

◆

To take advantage of shots inside 125 yards, you first need to have the right weapons to make it happen. I feel confident in saying you should carry at least three wedges, if not four, to have plenty of options from short range.

Here is a quick breakdown of the role of each wedge as part of your arsenal:

- **Pitching Wedge (PW)**: This club will come standard with any iron set and is between 43 and 46 degrees, depending on brand/model. It's great for full shots, knockdown shots, long bunker shots, and shots around the green.
- **Gap Wedge (GW)**: The next wedge is your gap wedge (also known as GW, AW, or UW). This is a club that many golfers forget about and it's a huge mistake. A gap wedge helps eliminate the "gap" between your pitching wedge and sand wedge. It's usually between 50 and 54 degrees and, overall, a very versatile club used in various ways.
- **Sand Wedge (SW)**: The SW is the most common wedge in the bag other than your PW. The loft is between 54 and 57 degrees and used for all kinds of shots inside 100 yards. For many golfers, this is the highest loft club in the bag.
- **Lob Wedge (LW)**: The last wedge you might want to carry is a lob wedge. While it's very versatile, it's difficult for higher handicap players to use.

Carry at least the first three wedges on this list. If you're a higher handicap player, you can skip the lob wedge for now and have an extra hybrid or high-lofted fairway wood instead. But as your game progresses, add a lob wedge to help with short-sided pitches and 50–70-yard shots.

Also, play the right set of wedges that match the rest of your set. For example, I see so many mid to high handicappers use heavy, unforgiving wedges that don't match their irons. The rest of their set is graphite, lightweight irons but their wedges are heavy steel shafts. This makes it hard to hit wedges consistently well and take advantage of the scoring zone.

Finally, make sure your wedges are spaced out equally or very close.

For example, if you carry three wedges, have six degrees between each to avoid huge yardage gaps. This might include PW (45), GW (51), and SW (57). If you opt to carry four wedges, the spacing will be *about* four degrees of loft between each club.

To become a wedge wizard, you need the right wand(s) to make it happen.

51. Use Bounce to make Better Contact

◆

Like most golfers, you might not understand what "bounce" is with your wedges. But you probably want to make better contact with your wedges and minimize hitting it thin or fat and instead find the middle of the club face.

Bounce can help with that. To take advantage of bounce, you need to first understand it. If you look at your sand wedge, you might see a few numbers like *56.08* or *55.10*.

Here's what that means and why it matters…

The first number refers to the <u>loft</u>, while the second number indicates the <u>bounce</u> on the wedge. Bounce refers to the angle created between the leading edge of the club and the trail edge. Essentially, it's the part of the wedge that sits on the turf.

Wedge bounce usually ranges between 4 and 12 degrees. This is important because some shots require more bounce while others need less. Using a wedge with the wrong bounce can make the shot a lot easier or harder.

Let's keep it simple—**bounce is your friend!**

One of the biggest mistakes in my own game was playing wedges with too little bounce. The result was a lot of thin, bad chip shots and horrific sand shots. When I switched to higher bounce, my short game improved overnight.

Ideally, you want a low, mid, and high bounce in your bag for different playing conditions.

- Low bounce is great for tight lies and firm conditions on the turf or in the sand.

- Mid bounce is great for normal playing conditions and a lot of greenside shots.
- High bounce is needed for thick, rough, fluffy lies and soft, fluffy sand.

Having an array of bounces makes it easier to hit different shots.

For example, when you find yourself in a bunker with fluffy sand, play a wedge with the most bounce and when you're on a bare lie around the green, play your wedge with the least bounce.

52. Weight Forward with Wedges

Once you have the right weapons in your bag, there is one rule for most wedge shots. One of the best things you can do at setup is getting more than half of your weight forward. I like to think, *weight forward with wedges*.

Keeping most of your weight on your lead leg ensures you hit down and through the shot. So many players try to scoop the ball and have too much weight on their back leg. But if you do this, the club will hit the ground, then the ball, resulting in a thin or skull shot.

Remember, wedges have 45 degrees of loft or more and they are meant to get the ball airborne; you don't need to help by scooping the ball up. Instead, you need to hit down on the ball so it will go up.

This is great advice for most situations but not all. In some lies, you will need to adjust, such as fluffy lies in the rough where the ball sits up, when your ball is on the upslope, soft sand, and other instances. But in general, for normal lies, having more weight slightly forward will help your contact immensely. Better contact will lead to closer proximity and hopefully, more up and down saves to keep the momentum going.

53. Always Accelerate

Like putting, you need to always accelerate with a wedge in your hand. Think about it like this, deceleration equals death.

I think so many golfers decelerate with wedges because of an outdated drill known as the clock drill. I will go against popular opinion and say the clock drill is one of the worst drills in the history of golf.

If you're not familiar with the drill, instructors suggest thinking of your swing like a clock. Each hand on the clock represents a part of your swing. That's why you might hear instructors on the range say, *"Take it back to nine or eleven o'clock,"* when they're teaching.

While the concept makes sense, it makes it easy to *decelerate* on the shot, which leads to all kinds of bad results.

If there's one concept I can't stress enough and want to end this section with, it's this—**always accelerate with a wedge in your hand**.

Whether you're hitting a chip, a pitch, a sand shot, or a wedge of any distance, always accelerate. This will ensure you don't flub a chip, leave your bunker shot in the sand, and make a quality strike with your wedges.

Plus, it will ensure you create the most backspin (even if the ball doesn't physically spin backward) as well. Remember, deceleration = death.

54. Dial in Two Distances for Each Wedge

♦

How far do you hit a pitching wedge? How about a sand wedge?

You probably know the carry number off the top of your head ... give or take a few yards. However, if you asked me, I would answer, *"Depends on the shot."*

Before I pull a wedge from the bag, I'm asking myself these questions:

- *What's the distance to the flagstick?*
- *How will this lie affect the clubface at impact?*
- *Where is the pin on the green (front, middle, back)?*
- *What's the wind doing? How about the temperature or elevation?*

It sounds like a lot, but as you play more frequently, asking these questions will become second nature. The reason I get so much data for each wedge is that this is the scoring zone.

To play your best golf, you need to take advantage when you have a wedge in hand.

While that doesn't mean you need to aim at the flag every time you have a wedge, you want to avoid bogeys from this position. You also want to give yourself an easy putt or chip if you do miss the green.

But don't feel like you should have a putt inside putter length anytime you have a wedge in hand. Despite what you might think, even the PGA Tour pros don't always stuff wedges (or even hit the green as often as you think).

→ **Wicked Smart Fact**

Look at the 2021 season PGA Tour average from normal different wedge distances:

Distance	Proximity from Fairway	Proximity from Rough
125–150 yards	23'2"	37'3"
100–125 yards	20'1"	31'7"
75–100 yards	17'6"	26'6"
50–75 yards	15'10"	25'5"

Plus, the average green in regulation percentage from inside 125 yards was 81%, meaning even the best players in the world miss greens with wedges!

When they do hit the green, the average distance is much longer than you might think. It's also crazy to see how the rough makes the proximity to the hole dramatically more.

Don't get me wrong; you need to know your full-swing distance with each club in the bag. But with wedges, you want to have at least two "stock" distances.

Because a lot of shots you'll face on the golf course aren't a full number—even if you gap your wedges three to four degrees apart. Often, the distance is between a pitching and gap or gap wedge and sand wedge.

That's why you need to have multiple distances for each wedge. When you have two stock distances with each wedge, things get lost easier in the scoring zone.

One is your "full" number, while the other is your "knockdown" or 3/4 swing number.

The knockdown number requires little other than choking down about an inch to an inch and a half. By shortening the club, you will lose some distance and gain some control. Plus, you should improve the strike and reduce the spin.

Once you get excellent and become a single-digit handicap player, aim for three distances for each wedge—a full number, a knockdown, and a distance where you choke up almost to the shaft.

55. Locate Your Landing Zone

When you miss the green and are chipping or pitching, you need a target, just like you do with full shots. I like to think of this as your landing zone; this is where you want the ball to land once it hits the green. It will change every time based on the shot, green conditions, break of the green, and more.

Your landing spot gives your mind something to focus on. Just like the full swing, you want to paint a clear picture of what you want from the shot, so your mind can make it happen. With chipping and pitching, you need a spot where you want the ball to land.

Unless you're extremely short-sided, make sure the landing zone is always on the green.

When you land a chip or pitch in the rough or the fringe, it's unpredictable and hard to tell how the ball will react. Sometimes it can bounce through the grass just fine, while other times it will get stuck in the rough and lead to you chipping again.

In general, I like to have my landing spot at least three to five feet past the fringe (if the pin position allows it). Otherwise, if you try to land it too close to the fringe and mishit it, your golf ball might hit the collar of the fringe and bounce forward. Fringe bounces are the worst as they kill any backspin and leave you with a much longer putt than if you hit the green first.

You can practice this pretty easily at the short game area. Take a small washcloth from home and make it your landing spot. Try to land as many chip or pitch shots as you can on the towel. Use a smaller landing spot like a quarter or poker chip ball marker as you get better.

Then, when you're on the golf course, try to imagine that marker or towel on the green. Try to find something that makes it easy to spot - an old cup, a discolored portion of the green, a poorly repaired divot, or something else. As part of your pre-shot routine, make that spot the last thing you look at, *not* the hole.

Too many golfers look at the hole last, which makes it more likely to hit it long and miss your spot. Remember, you need to plan for roll-out for each chip or pitch. Having a small, clear target on the course will help you get it up and down more often.

56. Forget the Flop

◆

Flop shots are sexy, but double bogeys are not.

The point?

Most amateurs try to make simple shots around the green 10X harder on themselves by getting the ball up in the air. Sure, it looks cool when your favorite PGA Tour player does it on TV, but it's not a high-percentage shot.

Instead, keep the shot low to avoid the big miss and blow-up hole.

There's nothing worse than hitting it by a par 4 in two shots only to walk away with six because of a terrible chip or pitch. As I mentioned in the putting section, always follow the rule: always make putting your first option around the green.

Remember, if you can't putt, chip it. If you can't chip it, then pitch it.

If this feels like I'm repeating myself, it's because I am. I can't stress this point enough.

When you do need to flop, here is my process to keep it simple:

- Ensure the lie allows the shot. If it's a bare lie or buried in the rough, skip the flop.
- Use your LW and set up with 70% of your weight on your lead foot. This will ensure you hit down on it and don't blade it.
- Choke up almost to the steel and make sure the face is open at address.
- The main thing to think about is speed as deceleration will lead to all sorts of trouble.
- Cock your wrists quickly and maintain your lower body throughout the swing.

57. Quit Fearing the Sand

When your ball disappears in a bunker, are you excited or terrified?

If you're like most golfers, I bet your stomach drops and you walk into the bunker with a ton of fear, constantly thinking about all the things that could go wrong in your quest to get the ball out of the sand. Trust me; I've been there myself.

I won't lie; the sand even scared me, despite being a scratch golfer for years. I think it was due to bad technique, no pre-shot routine, and scar tissue from many bad shots in the past. Horrible sand play led to me missing cuts, blow-up holes, and a few broken wedges.

At the time of publishing this book, I *think* my sand woes are fixed (knock on wood).

Before getting into the basics to help you get out of the sand every time, it's important to keep things in perspective. So many golfers think they are supposed to always get out and stick it close when they're in the bunker.

But if the pros don't, why should you expect yourself to be a wedge wizard from the sand?

→ **Wicked Smart Fact**

According to the PGA Tour, during the 2021 season, the best players in the world only got it up and down from the sand 50.5% of the time. Yes, you read that right, only 50% of the time.

Don't forget, these are the best players, in the best sand possible, hitting onto the best greens and they only got one out of two shots up and down. Plus, their proximity to the hole in that event from the sand was 9'7"—just under 10 feet!

So quit beating yourself up if you blade a bunker shot into the lip or chunk just onto the green.

Now that your expectations are reset, here are my basics for getting out of the sand:

- Use an SW or LW, preferably one with the most bounce (unless it's hard-packed sand, in which case you want less bounce). Open the clubface; this is the most important thing to do!
- Set up with the ball on your left heel with 70% of your weight on your lead foot.
- Set up square (not left) of the target. I like to open my shoulders but keep my feet square and this has made a huge difference in my contact.
- Match your shoulders with the slope (if any), so the club moves with the slope.
- Hit one 1–1.5 inches behind the ball. Remember, you aren't hitting the ball; you are hitting the sand, which carries the ball on to the green. The closer you hit to the ball, the more spin you will generate, but you also risk hitting it thin. Conversely, if you hit it more than two inches behind the ball, you will probably hit it fat and leave it in the bunker.
- Accelerate through the shot. Don't forget, sand is heavy, so you need speed to get the wedge through the sand.

Finally, all these tips will help you escape the sand, but don't forget to still go through a pre-shot routine and commit to a landing area. Also, if the sand scares the hell out of you, practice enough to where it's no longer a weakness!

Greg Norman once said, *"Spend two hours in a bunker. Two hours is all it takes to raise yourself out of the fear-and-doubt group (about 90 percent of all golfers) to the point where you can play from sand with confidence."*

58. Make Practice Difficult

When you spend time at the short game area, make practice hard ... like really hard. Try to give yourself lies that if they happened on the course, you would ask the Golf Gods, *"What did I do to deserve this?"*

The harder you can make practice, the easier it is when you're out on the golf course.

Think about it, rarely do we find ourselves on the course with flat, perfect lies where the ball is sitting up on a pillow. Yet, that's the conditions that most golfers practice from. This type of practice won't prepare you for when you're actually on the golf course.

Instead, practice the hard shots where the ball is above/below your feet, the ball is sitting down in the rough, or you're short-sided. While the goal is to hit each shot close, you also need to learn how different lies impact the trajectory and spin.

Think of short game shots like one giant experiment so that when you're on the course, you're prepared for anything. The more you can hit these shots in practice, the more you can trust your short game in big moments.

59. The Science of Spin

◆

Let me guess, you want to learn how to hit high wedges that soar into the heavens, hit the green, and zip back close to the flagstick?

Because let's get real, the shot looks sexy, you feel like a PGA Tour pro, and your playing partners are left in awe.

The truth is I hate backspin.

It's a huge pain. There's nothing more frustrating than hitting a perfect wedge you think will be a tap-in only to watch it suck back off the green. Now, suddenly, you're trying to get it up and down for par instead of tapping in a birdie putt.

Don't get me wrong, spin is helpful the majority of the time. It's nice when you hit a shot well and know how it should spin once it hits the green.

So, what's the secret to spin?

Speed.

Backspin comes from speed above all else and speed usually comes from full shots, which come from accelerating through impact (remember, deceleration = death to your shot).

Therefore, it's a lot easier to get backspin from 100+ yards vs. 30 or 40 yards. When you're closer to the green and can't take a full swing, it's nearly impossible to get the ball to spin backward or stop quickly. While it might hit, skip, and stop, anything inside about 75 yards won't spin back unless there is a huge contour in the green or conditions are very soft.

So if you want backspin, make sure you have a full swing above all else. You will not get the ball to spin back from greenside chips or 20-yard pitches. While they can stop quickly, spinning back only happens from farther back.

Then make sure you:

- Clean your grooves consistently.
- Play a ball that matches your swing speed and allows you to create spin.
- Have a good lie in the fairway. A tight lie makes it much easier to get juice and consistent spin. While the rough is much harder to create spin as grass will get interfere with making proper contact.

Lastly, make sure to buy new wedges more than any other club in your bag. I once read that Tiger Woods uses brand-new wedges every single week so he has optimal spin rates! While an iron set can last a few years, wedges should get replaced much more frequently.

60. The Dreaded 40–60-Yard Shots

The 40–60-yard shot is tough, even if you play frequently. This shot requires a lot of feel and it's easy to decelerate, which, as you know by now, leads to all kinds of bad shots. Plus, you won't have a full swing from this distance, so you won't get as much spin.

Here's a great example. During a one-day qualifier in 2017, I hit a poor drive in a fairway bunker off the first tee. I hit a decent shot out of there but wasn't wicked smart about my layup distance. I left myself an awful distance—65 yards to a front pin—and the greens were firm.

My first hole nerves were still in full effect and I decelerated and bladed my wedge into the water behind the green. I made double bogey on an easy par five and shot myself out of the tournament on the first hole. Yikes!

During my next lesson, I asked my coach for some help and said, *"How do you play a sixty-yard shot to a front pin?"*

His answer was simple. *"Don't leave yourself a sixty-yard shot to a front pin. That's just bad course management."*

While the truth hurts, he's not wrong either. If possible, don't leave yourself this shot because it's one that even the best golfers on the planet struggle with. But it's still golf and no matter how well you plan things, you're bound to find yourself in that awkward position occasionally.

Here's my simple strategy for this challenging distance, depending on pin location:

- **Front pin**: When the pin is up front and you're at this awkward distance, err on the side of caution. The middle of the green with a putt is better than leaving it short and having to get it up and down. I

like to play this shot with a lob wedge, with 70% of my weight on my front leg and choke up, nearly to the steel. I might open the face a little (depending on the lie) but aim to carry it at the pin and plan for a little release.
- **Middle pin**: With a middle pin, the shot isn't as intimidating because you have the most options. You can use a lob wedge, choke up and hit it half or three quarters. Or you can even use a sand wedge and flight it down. Like the front pin, make sure most of your weight is on the lead foot to ensure you hit down on the ball.
- **Back pin**: Finally, a back pin is not that hard from this tricky distance. I prefer a sand or gap wedge with this pin position as it's hard to get lob wedges close. An LW can check up too fast and leave you with a long putt. Instead, a GW or SW will skip more once it hits the green and releases to the back flag. With this shot, play it more in the center to slightly back in your stance. I also like to add a little more forward press before taking the club away to help add more forward spin (this also works when you're hitting chip shots around the green).

Bonus Video

Don't forget to watch the bonus materials at www.wickedsmartgolf.com/book to recap becoming a wedge wizard and my favorite drills.

Section V: Playing Wicked Smart Golf

Learn how to think your way around the golf course so you can go low (even on bad days)

Golf is a stupid game; one day, you can hit it great, and less than 24 hours later, all hell can break loose and it feels like you've never played golf in your life. Even if you're the best player in the world, your swing will disappear on some shots and some days entirely.

For amateurs, the act of a vanishing swing happens more than we care to admit. Sometimes it happens on the same day; your swing is on fire during your pre-game warm-up, but it disappears once you hit the course.

The bad news is that there is no answer—that's just golf. But the good news is you don't need your swing to always be "ON" to shoot your best scores. I like to think of this as being "wicked smart." While some people think of this as course management, this section will take it up a notch.

I've had countless numbers of rounds where I slapped it around but still broke 80, shot in the mid-70s or even broke par. Learning to *think* your way around the golf course (aka course management) is an art form. There's something special about not having your swing but still scoring well.

So, how do you shoot low scores even if your swing is off? It's a combination of everything we've put together so far; *mastering your mindset, practicing like a pro, finding peace with your putter and becoming a wedge wizard.*

When you master your mindset, you won't worry about bad shots or bad swings. You'll accept them, move on, and stay in the present moment.

Your game is more well-rounded when you have been practicing like a pro (and not an amateur). You'll have more shots in the bag, not as many technical swing thoughts dragging you down, and know your swing better.

When you're a great putter and have a solid putting routine, it'll be there to save the day on bad ball-striking days. Your putter will become your secret weapon to help you with par saves.

Finally, your wedges and shots around the green can help make it easier on your putter. You need this foundation to become a wicked smart golfer.

But the main thing you need to do is quit fighting your swing on bad ball-striking days. So many golfers play their swing on the golf course instead of playing golf! When you're on the golf course trying to make mechanical swing changes, it can make for a long day. It leads to tons of indecision, doubt, and fear of what might happen.

The golf course is not the place to work on your swing. Save that for the driving range after the round or the next day.

Instead of fighting against your swing, you need to play with what you have that day. Just accept it and use the tips in this section to play golf. It's about plotting your way around the golf course to give yourself more chances at your strengths.

Remember, your swing doesn't need to be "ON" to play great golf. You need to learn how to become resourceful and play with what you have. Trust me; the Golf Gods will reward you for playing hard, even if your ball striking is off.

61. Get The Right Gear

◆

Playing wicked smart golf and becoming an expert at course management starts *before* you get to the course. It starts by ensuring you have the right equipment for your swing and skill level to give you the best chance for success. Otherwise, you're making golf much harder on yourself.

Here are five things you want to think about when assessing your current equipment:

Buy a Rangefinder with Slope

Before playing the right clubs, you need to invest in a rangefinder or golf GPS with slope features. While you can't use slope in tournaments, you can use it in casual rounds and can help you hit better approach shots. I bet you will be shocked by how many greens are uphill or downhill, which can change your approach shot entirely.

Even if you play the same course over and over again, always use your rangefinder with slope. It's so easy to get lazy, assume you know the distance to certain holes, and then wonder why you're always short or long of the green.

Don't make golf harder by not knowing the proper distances for each shot. Because even if you hit the shot perfect, if your distance calibration is off, you won't get rewarded.

Play the Right Clubs

Pride and ego have ruined many golfers. Far too many golfers play clubs that don't match their ability, making a hard game nearly impossible. Hybrids, utility irons, and fairway woods make the game so much easier. You probably don't need a 3 or 4 iron (or maybe 5 iron yet) in your bag. Put the alpha male pride aside and play clubs that make it easier to hit more consistent shots. Let's face it; long irons are hard to hit, even for the best players in the world.

While golf legends probably wouldn't approve of these more forgiving clubs, you need them in your bag. I don't care about what clubs I play if they help me shoot lower scores.

For starters, your clubs need to match your skill level. Do not play clubs that look good or play a brand that your favorite PGA Tour pro plays.

Play the clubs that match your game and swing!

I can't give one specific recommendation as every player is unique, but it makes a big difference. While you don't need to get professionally fitted or buy new clubs every year, the right set can make golf a little bit easier.

Also, mix and match clubs from different brands. Too many amateurs think they should play all Callaway, Titleist, or Ping when I can almost guarantee with 99.99% certainty that one brand isn't the way to go. Even most PGA Tour pros who are sponsored don't play all 14 clubs from one brand. Instead, they play the ones that give them confidence and help them achieve the launch monitor metrics they want.

For example, I play Callaway woods and irons, but Titleist wedges and driving iron with a PXG putter. Don't feel like you need to play one brand just to look cool, play the ones that make golf more fun and easier to score.

Have More Hybrids and Forgiving Clubs

The everyday golfer has no business playing long, hard-to-hit irons. Instead, carry more hybrids, utility irons, and fairway woods. I used to carry a 7-wood in my bag in high school and loved that club. Despite getting tons of grief, that club rescued me more times than I can count.

Ironic enough, I just put another in my bag nearly 20 years later to attack par 5's. If it works and makes golf easier, play it!

Aside from easy-to-hit hybrids and high-lofted fairway woods, don't forget about wedges too. I see a lot of mid-to-high handicappers play the right irons but the wrong wedges.

For example, if you have a graphite shaft, cavity back irons, you need similar wedges. Yet, a lot of golfers play heavy, hard-to-hit wedges better suited for low-handicap golfers. You want your wedges like your irons, so it's an easy transition to them.

Remember, it's not about what brand of clubs you play or what clubs make up your set; it's the score tallied up after 18 holes that matters. Do not let pride make you buy clubs that make golf harder!

Swing the Right Shafts

Another aspect of your clubs to consider is the shafts. They play a pivotal role in your golf game, but most amateurs overlook this entirely. I would argue that using the right shafts is just as important as the clubs themselves!

Generally, most golfers play club shafts that are too heavy or stiff. This is a recipe for disaster, even if you have the right clubheads. Shafts that are too heavy or stiff limit your swing speed, which doesn't allow you to hit it as long. Plus, they are harder to swing later in the round and can result in injury too. And if you use shafts with too much flex, you will lose out on accuracy.

As you continue to develop your skills, increase swing speed, make swing changes, etc., keep upgrading your gear. Plus, a professional fitting is a great idea as you can test out different clubs and shafts with a launch monitor. This will help you avoid buyer's remorse and play the ideal clubs for your swing.

Get the Right Grips

Finally, don't forget about playing the right grips either. Since your hands are the only thing connecting you with the club, it's important to play grips that match your hand size and normal playing conditions.

So often I'll play with golfers who have different grips and different sizes throughout their bag. Let me tell you, this isn't making golf any easier. If you look at elite amateurs and professionals, they all play the same grip on their wedges, irons, and woods. Plus, they make sure to regrip before the grip itself affects their grip on the club.

Like so many parts of this section, these are all aspects of the game that are within your control. So use it to your advantage so you can play your best golf!

62. Get a Game Plan

◆

Once you have the right gear, you need a game plan to attack the golf course. Since caddies aren't the norm in most courses, you need to prepare for the round independently. There are a few ways you can do this:

Google Earth: If you've never played a golf course before, Google Earth is your best friend. You can get a good overview of the course, notice the layout of certain holes, and avoid trouble. Plus, you can map out landing distances, find the width/depth of the green, the fairway, and spot the best places to miss. Not to mention, it's 100% free!

GPS Devices: While most players have rangefinders, a golf GPS might be more helpful. A GPS handheld device, app on your phone, or golf watch can help you get a game plan for each hole. These devices will provide a flyover view of the hole, help you navigate hazards, find the best landing spots, and even help with the slope of the greens. While some golf carts have GPS devices, I wouldn't trust them with 100% certainty. While they're good to preview the hole, the distances aren't always correct to the pin and oftentimes are programmed to the middle of the green. A rangefinder and/or a golf GPS are better choices to play wicked smart.

Yardage Books: If you prefer to go the old-school route like me, yardage books are great. Most courses have basic yardage books in the pro shop and you can buy them on third-party websites as well. These are great because you can add notes from past rounds, which clubs you used, notate slope, wind, and more.

Rangefinder: Finally, a rangefinder is better than nothing and can help you navigate the course. I like to use my rangefinder with a yardage book to create a solid game plan for each hole.

Having one or several of these tools will help you create a solid game plan for the round and each hole. Don't waste strokes by not showing up prepared, as this is something you can easily control!

63. Warm Up to Win the Round

To play wicked smart golf, you need to set yourself up to win. That means playing the right clubs, creating a game plan for the round, and warming up properly. So many golfers skip a proper warm-up and then wonder why they struggle with the green speed or a bad front nine.

While you don't need to get there two hours before your tee time like the pros, you want to get there 30–60 minutes early. This will allow you to get into the right mindset, warm-up properly on the driving range, and test the greens. When you step on the first tee box, you will have tons of confidence and know that you did everything to set yourself up for a great day.

Here is what you should do before every round of golf:

- **Stretch and warm-up**. This will help you loosen up your golf muscles, avoid injury, and get ready to hit golf balls.
- **Warm-up slowly**. After stretching, don't go straight to hitting drivers. Start with easy wedges, full wedges, irons, and then woods. Work your way up slowly to let your body adjust.
- **Learn the speed of the greens**. While warming up on the driving range is important, spending time on the putting green is equally important. Spend a lot of time on two-to-six-footers to build confidence by seeing the ball go in the hole. Then hit longer putts to a ball marker or to the fringe to test the speed on different length putts.

You also want to use specific clubs in a pre-round warm-up, so it becomes a ritual. It should become automatic when you show up to the course to play. This will alert your mind that it's not just a normal practice session and that you're here to play and score well.

Here's my pre-round warm-up routine when playing in competitive events:

- Arrive at least 60 minutes early.
- Head straight to the putting green. Work on short putts and feel out the speed of the greens. I prefer to putt to tees or ball markers, no holes, as I want to emphasize speed as I get the speed dialed in. Then I'll put a bunch of 3-5 footers to see the ball find the bottom of the cup. Total time = 15 minutes.
- Chip, pitch, and sand shots = 10 minutes.
- Next up is the driving range. I always hit the same clubs before each round (in this order) SW, PW, 8 iron, 4 iron, 3W, and driver. When I'm hitting woods, I'll hit some wedges to maintain a good tempo. During my last few shots, I'll pick targets and go through my full pre-shot routine as if I were on the golf course. Total time = 25 minutes.
- Back to putting green for five minutes and go through my full putting routine with one golf ball.

I do this every single round. During casual rounds, I still do the same routine but spend less time on each part so it only takes 30–40 minutes.

Test out different routines and find what works best for you. Remember, it's all about building confidence and getting ready to attack the golf course.

Also, before the round is not the time to work on your swing with training aids and new swing thoughts. Save that for driving range sessions when you aren't playing. Trying to change your swing right before a round makes it hard to trust your swing on the golf course!

A good pre-round warm-up need not be long to be effective either (just like a good practice session). My recommendation is always set aside at least 30 minutes for an adequate pre-round warm-up. This way, you can stretch, hit balls, test out the speed of the greens, and set yourself up for success. Rushing to the first tee while skipping the range and practice green usually leads to disaster on the course. It's an easy tip that can make a huge difference in your game.

64. Always Analyze the Shot

Once you're on the golf course, it's time to *think* like a wicked smart golfer. The first thing you should do on any tee box or approach shot is to analyze the shot.

Here's an example of what I do for an approach shot:

- First, I evaluate the lie of the golf ball and the shot itself. I might step into the shot to see if my stance is uphill/downhill/sidehill and check to see how the ball is sitting. Is it in the rough? Fairway? Mud on the golf ball?
- Once I understand the lie and determine how the golf ball is sitting, I use my rangefinder to get the distance to flag. Then I factor in conditions such as wind, elevation of the golf course, slope, and weather.
- Then I determine where I want the shot to go—hint: it's rarely at the flag. Unless I have a wedge, I am rarely aiming at the flag and instead go towards the widest part of the green. I find where I want to hit and where I want to avoid (aka, a bad miss) that will leave me short-sided and a tough up and down.
- Once I have all things considered for the shot, I pick a number I want the golf ball to carry. Please note this is not the flag distance! You need to plan for roll, wind, and the lie. So if I have 150 yards to the flag with some wind behind me, I want to hit it 144 yards.
- Finally, I pick the club that will help me hit that shot and find my two targets.

While it might sound like a lot, this process will become automatic after enough repetition. This seems simple, but so many golfers skip assessing the lie and factoring in the wind or where to hit. Then they short side themselves and invite big numbers into the hole.

Always analyze your shot, so you pick the right club for the job and minimize unnecessary errors.

65. Stay Loyal to Your Pre-Shot Routine

◆

Once you have a clear number for the shot, it's time to go through your routine. Developing and sticking with a pre-shot routine is one of the easiest ways to play better golf.

If you watch any golf on TV, you will see that each player has their own routine. While no two routines are the same, each player has their own, and it helps them build confidence over any shot.

Once you develop and hone your pre-shot routine, it's incredible how much more confident you will feel over the golf ball, especially when you want to hit a great shot in a tournament or have money on the line. Your pre-shot routine is your gateway to *"The Zone"* or, as Helen Alfredsoson described it, getting into a cocoon.

In your cocoon, time stands still and nothing else matters but the shot at hand. A hundred percent of your focus is on the shot you face. When you get in there, it's a beautiful feeling. But when players don't stick to their pre-shot routine, things can go south quickly.

Here's a perfect example. Tiger Woods, known by many to have one of the strongest mental games ever, has a consistent pre-shot routine. Scott Fawcett, creator of Decades Golf, found that when Tiger was at his best, his pre-shot routine was the same length of time every swing - each routine was within milliseconds of each other. His pre-shot routine was automatic and helped him get into the zone or the cocoon.

Here's another example—Greg Norman. While he's a very accomplished player with two major championships and 20 PGA Tour wins, he had a tough meltdown at the Masters in 1996.

If you watch the footage, one thing is for sure, he's not comfortable on the course that day. While Augusta tends to do that to even the best players, Greg didn't stick to his pre-shot routine. It's noticeably different on that fateful Sunday at the Masters and might have helped contribute to a final round 78 that led to his collapse.

As Nick Faldo, his playing partner and eventual winner of the 1996 Masters said, *"I could feel the nervousness emanating from Greg. He gripped and regripped the club, as though he could not steel himself to hit the ball."*

Don't get me wrong; a pre-shot routine won't save you from a bad day on the course, but it can help you tremendously. A consistent pre-shot routine can help you calm down, stay focused, and not get ahead of yourself to play your best golf.

66. Only Think About Your Target

♦

When you're on the course, you have one thing and one thing only to think about. Hint—it's NOT your score. It's your target!

One of the most important parts of solid course management and playing wicked smart golf is focusing only on your target. Dr. Bob Rotella said it best in his book, *The Golfer's Mind*. *"The more you're consumed with your target, the more your instincts and subconscious will help you find it. It's as if you have an automatic guidance system and the ball is your missile."*

As I mentioned in the pre-shot routine lesson (#22), you should have two targets for full-swing shots. The first target is where you want the ball to end up in the fairway or green. When choosing a target in the distance on the golf course, I like to find something obvious and will stick out.

I like to pick targets like a specific tree, a power line, an electrical box, a maintenance shed, or something else that's obvious. The vaguer and broader the target, the more difficult it is to confirm your target in your pre-shot routine. Find something that is easy to spot in the distance so you can stay in the zone as you're standing over the golf ball.

The second target is directly in front of your golf ball (an intermediary target) that lines up with the long-range target. Having an intermediary target is so important because it ensures that your club face is set up square to your long-range target. Even for great players, it's nearly impossible to square up the face to a target that is hundreds of yards away. That's where the intermediary target comes in.

Once you select your long-range target, draw an imaginary line back to your golf ball. Then, a few feet ahead of your ball, locate an intermediary target. This is usually a spot of grass, the edge of a divot, or something else that makes it easy to square up the face.

Once you have the face square to the short target, you can also ensure you're aligned to the long-range target. Like a missile, once you're locked on, that's the only thing you want to think about until your swing is complete.

67. Quit Caring About Your First Shot of the Day

I probably don't have to tell you that the first tee jitters are real and we already covered how to reframe nerves on the first tee. But now that we're focused on playing wicked smart golf on the course, I want to emphasize that the first shot or first hole does not dictate the rest of the round.

I've had some very nervous first tee shots in my career, my first tournament shot after taking eight years off competitive golf, my failed college tryout, and some high-level amateur events. But nothing compares to the nerves I felt at my first shot at pre-qualifying Q-school in 2019.

If you don't know, Q-school is the formal process to professional golf on the Korn Ferry Tour, which is a stepping stone to the PGA Tour. To earn status on the Korn Ferry Tour, you need to make it through four stages over a few months on difficult golf courses. It's an expensive and tedious process.

I had flown to Nebraska a few days earlier and was one of a handful of amateurs in the event. From the moment I woke up, I had so much anxiety, and I'm not even sure I slept as I was so nervous and excited. When my time finally came and the starter said, "*Now playing, from Scottsdale, Arizona ... Michael Leonard,*" my heart nearly exploded out of my chest.

I was so nervous and excited I felt like my heart could explode. But I reframed my nerves, told myself I'm excited, and stuck to my pre-shot routine. Luckily, I did much better than my college tryout but hit a lackluster thin, pull cut 3-wood that somehow found the fairway. It only went about 70% of its normal distance, but I was off and running in the biggest event of my life. Then I hit an awful wedge over the green, stubbed a chip, and had to make a 10-footer for bogey.

Luckily, I avoided a dreaded double on one of the easiest holes on the course and calmed my nerves. Despite a horrible first tee shot and hole, I shot an even par 71 in my biggest competitive round ever.

The point?

Your first tee off means nothing, nor does your first hole.

I've striped drives down the middle of the fairway and walked off the first green with a double bogey. I've also hit awful opening drives that left me feeling embarrassed and went on to make a birdie.

That's just golf.

Your first tee shot and first hole do NOT set the tone for your round unless you allow them to. Remember, each shot counts the same on the scorecard; don't let the first few swings hinder playing your best golf.

68. Never Trust Tee Markers

Greenskeepers set you up to fail often and most golfers don't even realize it. Sometimes it's intentional on their part and other times it just happens with no conscious effort. You might be thinking, how so?

By not double-checking the tee markers are aimed at the fairway.

Whether you realize it or not, some tee boxes align with the fairway or green, but other times they point in a different direction. A lot of times they'll have them pointed toward trouble or rough instead of the fairway. If you don't focus during your pre-shot routine, it's easy to aim at trouble and not at your ideal target.

For example, sometimes the tee markers will point to the straight part of the fairway even if it doglegs to the right. If you're not careful, it's easy to line up to the tee markers, not your intended start line. In this instance, you could hit it dead straight but end up going through the fairway into the rough or other trouble.

Whether intentionally or unintentionally, this can wreak havoc on your tee shot and make it harder to score well by putting you out of position from the start of the hole. Then, the rest of the hole you're playing defense, not offense. Always make sure that you pick your own target on every tee box, don't just mindlessly aim parallel to the tee boxes.

69. Club Up On Approach Shots

◆

Whether you realize it or not, most trouble is short of the green. While some holes might have a bunker or water behind the green, most of the trouble is short.

Why?

Because greenskeepers know that most golfers end up short and thus place the trouble strategically. Here are two reasons most golfers miss the green short more than long:

- **Not knowing distances**: Most golfers think they hit it further than they do. They try to muscle a club that will only get to the green if it's struck perfectly (which is rare for a lot of golfers). This is why it's so important to spend time on the driving range or in a simulator dialing in your distances. When you have a baseline for each club, it's easier to get your ball to the hole and not end up where most of the trouble is.
- **Most greens are slightly elevated**: Aside from not taking enough club in the first place, most greens are elevated, even if just by a few yards. But a few yards can make a big difference, which leads to not taking enough club and, once again, ending up short. Even relatively flat courses can have a few yards of elevation change that aren't seen to the naked eye. This is why I always recommend investing in a rangefinder with a slope feature so you can see this firsthand.

If you're between clubs, pick the longer one in general (unless there is trouble long). Try not to use the club that you must hit 100% perfectly to reach the green. If you hit it great, you should have an easier chip shot. If you don't hit it great (which will happen most of the time for the average player) you should still have a putt.

After learning more course management inside the Decades Golf program, the numbers show that missing long is almost always better than short. This should cause more looks for birdies so you can score consistently better.

Remember, golf is a game of misses. Play for the misses, not the perfect shots as they don't happen nearly as much as we'd like.

70. Pre-Set to Play With Confidence

Confidence, confidence, confidence; we all want it over every shot we face. There's nothing worse than being over a shot and thinking, *I have no clue how to pull this off.*

This is yet another reason I love golf so much. Every time you tee it up, you're bound to get new challenges, whether your perfect drive ends up in a divot, your pin-seeking approach hits the flag and rolls off the green, or some other scenario.

While you can practice all you want on the driving range, some shots are nearly impossible to work on in practice. Sometimes you just have to feel it out when you're on the course. But that might lead to some anxiety as you've never executed the shot.

To help you feel more confident over tough shots, try out pre-setting.

This practice is simple… step into the shot as if you were about to pull the trigger. Get into your normal stance, grip the club, and stand over the ball just like you will soon do. This will help make your brain gain more confidence with the shot and it won't feel so foreign when you do need to get up and hit the shot or putt.

For example, if I have a shot where the ball is well above or below my feet, I always pre-set. I'll go up to the ball and set up as if I'm about to hit the shot. This allows my body to feel my setup by choking up on the club if it's above my feet or flexing my knees if it's well below my feet. It also helps my mind see the target and imagine the shot I'm trying to hit. Then I'll back off and go through my normal pre-shot routine.

I also like to pre-set or long putts or other challenging putts with multiple breaks or tiers. It helps me find my start line and not feel as anxious about the putt once I'm standing over the real thing.

Pre-setting allows you to mentally prepare for the shot, so the shot doesn't feel that intimidating when you need to pull the trigger. The cool thing is this works for all parts of your game and it's easy to do. Pre-set to ease your mind and body, so you're prepared for the shot.

71. Minimize Mechanical Swing Thoughts

◆

The next time you watch the PGA Tour, listen to what the players say after a good round in their post-round interviews. They will usually say things like, *"I was just focused on my target,"* or, *"Stuck to my game plan,"* or something along those lines.

Never do you hear them say, *"I was thinking about taking the club outside on the takeaway and dropping it in the slot on the downswing,"* or, *"All day, I was focused on strengthening my grip, pausing at the top, and holding my follow through."*

You can't play your best golf when you're constantly thinking about your swing.

Technical swing thoughts do not belong on the golf course; they belong on the driving range. It's up to you to train your swing in practice so you trust it on the golf course.

When you think about your swing technically, you block the magic of going unconscious on the golf course. It's easy to play tight as the conscious mind is overly active. But remember, the subconscious is where greatness comes from.

In the book *Be a Player*, Pia Nilsson and Lynn Marriott break down the importance of each part the brain plays. They say, *"Here's an important fact. The cognitive center of the brain comprises a minuscule 5 to 10% of our brain power. The reactive side comprises 90 to 95% - much of which we never access."*

Ideally, you want to limit yourself to one technical swing thought—at most to activate the "reactive side" of your brain. Any more than one swing thought and it's like negotiating with a terrorist while you're standing over a shot.

Remember from section one, your mind can destroy a good round before you ever begin your takeaway. Focus on your target and swing your swing to play your best golf.

72. Understand How to Play Uneven Lies

◆

As you can tell in this section, practicing your golf swing on the range vs. playing golf on the course is very different.

On the driving range, you get to hit from flat lies, good grass, and clear targets, which is ironic because it's rare to get flat lies with perfect grass out on the course. You're more likely to find some mud on your ball, uneven lies, rough, sand, and more.

To play your best golf, you need to learn how to adjust to different lies on the course. Even if you can't practice these shots (unless you're doing on-course practice), knowing *how* to hit them will increase your chances of success.

Before sharing the best ways to adapt to different situations on the course, I think it's all about setup more than swing changes. For example, let's say your ball ended up on a hill and it's well above your feet. Many right-handers assume you need to take the club further inside on the backswing to compensate for the lie. This leads to extra swing thoughts instead of playing golf instinctively.

I would argue that you need to change your setup more than your swing with uneven lies. If it's extremely uphill, sidehill, or downhill, you *might* need to change your swing, but adjusting your setup is much easier. Plus, it allows you to focus on playing golf vs. thinking about swing changes on the course. You don't need to change your grip either. Instead, change your setup to accommodate the uneven lie.

Here is how the ball will react to different lies and how to adjust on the golf course to hit it well. For any of these lies, the longer the club, the more the ball will react off the lie. So if you find yourself with a drastically altered lie, less club is usually the play to not invite a big miss into the hole.

Uphill Lie

When your ball is on the upslope, it will launch higher, which means you will likely need to club up. The more the upslope, the higher it will go and the less distance it will travel.

For uphill shots, the main thing you want to do is adjust your shoulders to the slope. This will allow you to swing with the slope and not dig the club into the ground. You can also move the ball slightly up in your stance as well.

Last, aim right of your target as the ball comes out left from uphill shots.

Downhill Lie

When your ball is on the downward slope, it will launch lower, so you will likely need to club down. The more the downward slope, the lower it will go and the extra distance it will travel.

For downhill shots, you also want to adjust your shoulders to the slope. This will allow you to swing with the slope and not hit the ground before hitting the golf ball. You can also move the ball slightly back in your stance to make better contact.

Last, aim slightly left of your target as the ball comes out right from a downhill lie.

Ball above Your Feet

Sidehill lies are a little different from an uphill or downhill shot. When the ball is above your feet, the stance and lie will make your swing flatter, making it easier to draw the golf ball (assuming you're a right-handed golfer).

You need to choke up on the golf club to compensate for the slope to adjust. The more the ball is above your feet, the more you should choke up.

Plan for these shots to come out hot as you'll have a lot of topspin from the draw. Aim right of your target to account for the right-to-left ball flight.

Ball below Your Feet

When the ball is below your feet, the stance and lie will make your swing upright, making it easier to cut the golf ball. To adjust, you want to make sure to bend your knees to keep a stable base during your swing. Aim left of your target to account for the left-to-right ball flight.

If your ball is also in the rough and you're faced with one of these uneven lies, play even more conservatively. This isn't the time to get ultra aggressive and go flag hunting as these lies will affect your path and trajectory.

Hitting from Divots

Finally, if the Golf Gods test you and your ball gets stuck in a divot, don't panic. While it's frustrating, it's a part of the game. With a few simple setup adjustments, you can still make good contact.

Here's how:

- Put the ball slightly further back in your stance (think back-center, not off your back foot).
- At setup, put more of your weight on your lead foot (60% on your front foot) to hit down on the golf ball.
- Choke up on the club to get slightly steeper and hit the ball then the ground.
- Keep a low follow-through, sort of like a knockdown shot instead.

Finally, trust it and commit to the swing.

Uneven lies are part of golf and one of the reasons why it's so hard to practice on the range like you play on the golf course. That's why it's so important to play more golf and get yourself into these scenarios on the course, unlike a flat, perfect fairway lie at the driving range.

73. Playing Par 3s

◆

Each type of hole in golf requires different strategies. For example, par 3s might be the shortest and appear the easiest, but they're the hardest type of hole to score on.

→ **Wicked Smart Fact**: In the 2021 PGA Tour season, par 3s were the most difficult to score for the best players in the world.

- Par 3 Scoring Average: **3.08**
- Par 4 Scoring Average: **4.05**
- Par 5 Scoring Average: **4.60**

As you can tell, par 3s and 4s are played slightly over par while the pros dominate par 5s. With everyday golfers, this scoring average is often amplified and I see more double bogeys on par 3s than 4s or 5s, which is frustrating since you're leaving your driver in the bag.

To play better and shoot lower scores, you need to eliminate big numbers on short holes. **With par 3s you should have one goal, make a par.**

For mid-length to long par 3s aim for the widest part of the green, take a two-putt and run to the next hole. If it's a long and challenging hole, don't short-side yourself with your approach. You have a much better chance of getting it up and down when you have more green to work with.

For short par 3s where you have a wedge or short iron in hand, you can play slightly more aggressively if there isn't a ton of trouble. But the middle of the green will never hurt you. If your birdie putt goes in, great, but if not, a par will never hurt you.

74. Playing Par 4s

The strategy for par 4s is different; some par 4s are short and drivable but have some risk as well, while others require a perfect drive and long second shot just to get on the dance floor.

When it comes to par 4s, I think you should take the driver off the tee often but not every single time. For example, on short par 4s where you can drive the green, use a driver if there isn't a ton of trouble around the green.

For middle-length holes, a driver will give you a shorter approach shot, which should make it easier to find the dance floor. On long par 4s, you want as much distance as possible to have a shorter club in your hand and hopefully get on (or near) the green.

These are general guidelines I think you should adhere to but not a firm and fast rule. Some holes set up well to your eye with a driver while others don't and hit a 3-wood.

When you're unsure which club to hit on a par 4, always think about the second shot. Think about where you want to play from in your approach to the green.

A par will not hurt your score on par 4s either - remember, the best players in the world even score slightly over par on them. While it's great to make birdies on the short ones, don't press the issue by hitting the driver when there is a lot of trouble around the green.

75. Playing Par 5s

Par 5s might be the longest type of hole but statistically they're also the easiest to make eagles and birdies. These are the holes you need to take advantage of to play your best golf.

As I mentioned in the par 3 lesson, PGA Tour pros take advantage of par 5s with a scoring average of 4.60 in the 2021 season. I also love when I play a course with four reachable par 5s as I know I can make some magic.

Don't let the total distance of the hole scare you and instead, play one shot at a time. Sometimes you can get on or near the green in two or have a wedge in on your third shot. The goal with these holes is to make a par but hopefully, have plenty of good looks at birdie.

Here's my rule for most everyday players… if you hit a good drive and can get within 20 yards of the green with a good second shot, go for the green! It is not only more fun than laying up, your chances of making birdie go up significantly. I think, often, a 20–30 yard pitch (even from the rough) is easier than a shot from 100 yards in the fairway.

Finally, if you find yourself out of position after a poor drive, don't force a birdie by hitting an aggressive recovery shot. If you compound a bad second shot after a bad drive, you risk making a six or more on holes statistically the easiest holes. If you hit a bad drive, make it your goal to get back in play and give yourself the best opportunity to make par.

76. Middle of the Green Magic

To play your best golf, the middle of the green needs to become your best friend. If you dropped a ball on the middle part of the green on every hole for 18 holes and putted from there for a birdie, you would probably shoot even par or close to it. That's the magic of finding the middle of the green more often than not.

Yet, 90% of all golfers try to attack pins all the time thinking that's the only way to make birdies. Don't get me wrong; it's fun to take dead aim at the flag, but it's also how you short-side yourself and get more bogeys or doubles on your scorecard. When you're short sided, you have to play high pitch shots that are much more difficult to hit consistently vs. missing a green with tons of room and you can play a lower, bump and run type shot. Plus, they're just a harder shot to hit consistently, even if you have a world-class short game.

The key to playing better, more consistent golf is to avoid bogeys more than it is to make more birdies. And one of the main reasons most golfers card more bogeys and doubles is from playing too aggressively on approach shots.

Honestly, I wish that golf courses would forget to put flag sticks into the cups on certain days. I'm convinced that the everyday golfer would play better golf because it would force them to aim at the center or the widest part of the green. Then they would play better and see firsthand, not going for the pin is usually the right strategy.

Tiger Woods illustrated this perfectly when he won his fifth Masters in 2019. If you rewatch the footage on YouTube, you will see that Tiger almost never short sided himself. Despite being an incredible ball striker and his game was on fire, he always played away from the pin. And he walked away with the green jacket. It's not just the Masters either, that's his game overall and one of the secrets of his success. He rarely short sides himself and if he does, he has the short game to back it up.

Even as a scratch golfer I aim for the center of the green more often than not. The only time I go for the pin is if it's in the middle of the green or if I have a wedge or less into the green. Otherwise, I'm more than happy with finding the dance floor in the middle of the green.

Remember, golf is a percentage game; the more you're on the dance floor in regulation the more likely you are to make pars and birdies. Plus, the more often you're hitting birdie putts, the more you can feel the speed of the greens and eventually, some of those putts will find the bottom of the cup. So you just need to give yourself more opportunities instead of always trying to get up and down.

Sure, your friends will give you grief occasionally, but you'll get the last laugh when you beat them more often than not.

77. Ditch 3 Wood Off the Deck

◆

Aside from the driver, a 3 wood is the hardest club to hit from the turf. It's a long club, there isn't much loft, and even good players still hit some bad shots with it.

Yet, so many golfers try to hit 3 wood all the time because they think it will get them closer to the green. Sure, if you hit it well, it will get closer to the green than any other club in the bag. But the odds of the average golfer hitting it well isn't high. Plus, your misses are substantially bigger and can bring double bogeys or worse into play.

That's why I suggest hitting a 5 wood, 7-wood, or even subbing out your 3-wood for a 4 wood instead. A 4-7W all have much more loft and are 10X easier to hit from the deck. Unless you practice hitting 3W from the deck on the driving range consistently, don't do it. It's not a high percentage cost and usually requires a nearly perfect strike to make it worth it.

Take a club with more loft so you can hit it well, give yourself a better next shot, and keep your confidence going. There's nothing worse than topping a 3W and losing all your momentum in the round. Unless the lie is absolutely perfect, there isn't a ton of trouble, and you practice the shot consistently, skip it.

78. Play Conservatively When Your Swing Is Off

◆

Let's face it, swinging poorly sucks.

There's nothing worse than being excited about a round of golf only to go out there and seemingly forget how to swing. Sometimes it even happens after a great warm-up session too - the Golf Gods love to challenge us. But it's part of the game and something you need to learn how to deal with. Because no one is coming to save you mid-round, it's up to you to figure it out.

When most people swing poorly, they usually try to play more aggressively to make up for a bad hole or two. But this is the wrong idea and usually leads to more big misses off the tee and more short-sided shots around the greens, which usually lead to higher scores.

At times, you need to get conservative and play the shot you know that you can hit … not the one you hope you can pull off. After a few bad shots or a bad hole, you want to hit one good shot again to get your confidence back. This will positively snowball into more good shots and swings, but it all starts with one.

Here are a few ways to apply this on the golf course and not compound mistakes:

- **Play it safe off the tee.** One of the worst things you can do when your swing is off or you just made a big number is to swing like you're a long drive pro on the next tee shot. Often you're still mad, not thinking straight, and playing too aggressively can compound the mistake from the last hole. Take a club off the tee; you can swing hard (sometimes it's a driver but could be a 3W or hybrid) depending on the tee shot. While it's okay to swing a little more aggressively in these moments, stick to your pre-shot routine, pick a target, and commit to the shot. Fall back on the fundamentals!

- **Aim for the middle of the green.** Remember, the middle of the green is your best friend, especially if you need to bounce back from a bad hole and you don't feel great over the golf ball. Hit the shot you know you can hit and try to make par on your approach shot. If you make birdie, great, but don't force it. After a few consistent swings, you'll get your confidence back and give yourself more birdie opportunities.
- **Choke up when things are going bad.** If your swing has done the vanishing act, choke up and take an extra club on your approach shot. By choking up, you will make the club shorter and easier to control. By taking an extra club, you can focus on a smooth swing instead of trying to kill it.

79. Never Penalize a Perfect Shot

Don't you love it when you hit a perfectly straight shot? Whether it's a 7-iron or a driver, it feels amazing, because let's get real, it's the hardest shot to hit in golf. Well, that's what Tiger says and I take his word for it.

Let's say you slice the ball and have been hitting it left to right the entire round. On the par 4 11th, which has water down the left side, you aim at the edge of the water and play your slice ... only you hit it dead straight! Your perfectly straight ball just went for a swim and you must take a penalty shot. If you're like most golfers, you probably say, *"I've been slicing it all day, of course, this is the one time it didn't slice."*

When in reality, it's 100% your fault, as you penalized a straight shot!

Never penalize a perfectly straight shot.

In this example, you want to aim down the left center and play your trusty fade but never aim directly at a hazard. This is an easy course management error to help you save strokes all over the course.

80. Avoid the Dreaded Double Bogey

◆

Double bogeys (or worse) are absolute round killers.

A double bogey requires a few birdies to get those strokes back unless you make an eagle. It requires multiple holes of grinding away to make up for one bad hole. Meanwhile, a bogey can be replaced quickly with a birdie. But more than just trying to get those shots back, a double bogey kills momentum, which isn't easy to get in the first place.

One goal for every single round is to avoid double bogeys at all costs. If I hit a bad shot and find myself in the desert, behind trees, or some other obstacle, I ask myself, *How can I make bogey at worst?*

Asking yourself this question instantly shifts your mindset and removes an aggressive mindset that too many of us have during the round. If you're in trouble, do everything you can to give yourself a putt at par, don't try to force a birdie and end up walking away with a double bogey.

Quit trying to play hero golf.

Sometimes you have to take your medicine (aka a bogey) and move on to the next hole. But other times you need to stay mentally engaged when you find yourself in a tough spot too. As Arnold Palmer said in *My Game and Yours*, "*Most amateurs give up too quickly when they get into trouble. Every golfer should keep their eyes and mind open, looking for opportunities to do the unconventional.*"

When you hit a bad tee shot or poor approach shot, hit the shot you know you can play, not the one you think you can hit. Figure out how you can give yourself a putt at par and accept that a bogey won't kill you. Minimize the damage so you can save some momentum!

81. Give Up on Guiding Shots

We all have those holes that just make us uncomfortable. For example, imagine a tight fairway — water on the left side, tons of trees lining the right side.

When you don't like the way a hole sets up, it's easy to forget your pre-shot routine or get too technical with your swing. And if you're like most golfers, chances are you get tense and try to guide your swing on narrow fairways. I find this also happens on holes that just don't fit my eye like blind shots, doglegs, or quirky holes.

When a hole sets up weirdly, it's easy to try to guide the shot instead of swinging like normal. Instead, so many players (myself included) tend to swing easy in an attempt to steer it in the right direction. Trying to guide a shot almost never works well as you lose out on the natural, athletic motion you normally have in your swing. Plus, you're probably thinking too much and not focused on your routine and targets.

Caring about a shot doesn't mean you will hit it better, usually, it makes it worse. You need to trust yourself, your game, and play to hit a great shot. As Raymond Floyd said in *The Element of Scoring*, *"Good drivers swing with trust. Once your basic swing has proved that it can produce relatively straight shots, the way to give it its best chance to do so is to have faith in the centrifugal force of a freely swung clubhead."*

On tight holes, pick your target, a club you feel comfortable with, go through your pre-shot routine, and swing hard. Not overly hard like Bryson DeChambeau, but don't try to guide it either. Swing like normal, trust yourself, and accept the results. Nine times out of 10 you will hit a better shot when you swing with power and trust vs. swinging with fear and tension in your body.

Remember, it's just a golf shot.

82. Respect the Rough

Playing golf from the rough is part of the game - the PGA Tour driving accuracy average in the 2021 season was 60.69%. Meaning they only hit about eight of the 14 fairways in regulation. Playing from the rough is part of the game but requires its own strategy as it's very different from a fairway lie.

The rough makes approach shots much more difficult and the longer and thicker the rough, the more conservatively you should play. For the most part, this isn't the time to attack the flag as you can't predict spin like a fairway lie. Your ability to spin the ball changes drastically in the rough and sometimes, you will catch flier lies that will make the ball take off 10-20 yards longer than normal. Other times, your ball will nestle down in the rough and you'll have to chop down on it to get it out and will only travel a fraction of the normal distance.

If you remember an earlier example in the wedge section of the book, even the best PGA Tour players struggle from the rough. They hit fewer greens and are much further from the hole on average when compared to playing from the fairway.

The rough deserves respect. Don't try to play aggressively from the rough as you can compound a poor drive and bring double bogey into the hole way too easy.

Determine the Lie

The first thing to do when your ball is in the rough is to analyze the lie. Because you can hit a perfect shot but if you didn't understand how the lie would affect the shot, it won't matter. You always want to ask yourself, *Is this lie a flier or is it sitting down?*

A flier is when the ball is perched up on the rough nicely as if it's sitting on a pillow. This type of lie makes the ball carry extra distance (five to 15 or even 20 yards depending on the club used and length of the shot) and minimizes backspin. With a flier lie, you want to club down as the ball will travel farther and have less backspin.

Meanwhile, if the ball is sitting down in the rough, you want to do the exact opposite. You want to take more club and put the ball slightly back of center to hit down on it. This lie will also reduce spin, so play for more roll than normal. When the ball is nestled in the rough, the goal should be to bounce your approach shot up to the green or land it on the front edge. You also need to be careful about not taking too much club for a bad lie.

Open the Club Face

After you assess the lie, you need to make one setup adjustment to the clubface as the rough will twist it closed as you swing. The longer the rough, the more the club will twist and shut the face, leading to pulls and draws.

To offset the clubface closing, open the face at address position. The thicker the rough, the more you should open the face to account for the thick grass twisting the face shut at impact.

Finally, don't forget to add a little extra grip pressure as well. More pressure will also prevent the club face rotating too much through impact.

Play a Cut, Not a Draw

Since the rough naturally shuts the face, it's typically a good idea to play a fade vs. a draw from the rough. If you hit it well, it should be the right distance and work out well. Remember, you want to play toward the widest part of the green and rarely take dead aim at the flagstick from the rough (unless it's in the middle of the green).

Avoid Hitting Fairway Woods

Finally, to respect the rough don't make it a habit to hit long fairway woods very often, unless you have a perfect lie. Even if the ball is sitting up, sometimes it might go too far and sail over the green. If the lie does allow for a wood, make sure it's a 4, 5 or 7 wood (or hybrid) as hitting a 3-wood is very difficult to hit from the rough, even for low handicap golfers.

All of these tips should help you make better contact from the rough. After an errant drive, you need to respect the rough and play more conservatively than you would from the same distance in the fairway. Take your medicine, give yourself an opportunity to make par, and play more aggressively when you're back in the fairway.

83. Tee Away from Trouble

As I keep saying, to become a wicked smart golfer, you need to control what you can control. Where you tee up your golf ball on the tee box will help make the hole wider and easier than other places on the box.

For example, when there is out of bounds or water to the right, you obviously want to miss the left so you can avoid costly penalty strokes. To avoid the hazard, you want to open up the left side of the hole by teeing it up on the right side of the tee box. While it won't completely eliminate the hazard on the right, it will widen the hole as opposed to teeing it in the middle or left side of the box.

If the trouble is left, tee up on the left side and vice versa with the right side. Always tee up on the side of the box where the worst trouble is to widen the hole and give yourself the best opportunity. If there is trouble on both sides of the hole, tee up away from the one with a bigger penalty (ex. If there is water left and out of bound right, water is better than OB so tee up on the right side of the box).

But a lot of holes don't have much trouble so you might think the middle of the tee box is the right spot. Instead, you want to play the side that favors your typical shot shape. If you play a cut, tee up from the right side of the box to open up more of the left side to play a left to right shot shape. Conversely, with a draw you will want to tee up on the left side of the box to open up the right side of the fairway and allow for a right to left shot shape.

Don't forget, you have the option to tee up to two clubs behind the markers too. This might allow a better angle and help you feel more comfortable on the tee shot (or find a flat lie) so take advantage of it. This sounds easy but it's amazing how many golfers never think about tee box location and make it much harder to score consistently well.

84. Forget about the Flagstick

Rangefinders are a gift and a curse. While it's amazing that we have the technology to find our distance quickly from anywhere on the course, most golfers don't step back to analyze the shot after they get a distance. So many players get to their ball, laser the flag, pull a club, and go without thinking about the actual number they need to hit the shot.

After you get the distance to the flag, you need to consider:

- Lie
- Wind
- Total distance
- Best place to miss

The pin is one number but it's not THE number for 99% of shots.

Don't play the pin as you need to plan for the proper amount of release on each club. The longer the club, the more you need to plan for bounce as they won't have as much spin. With shorter irons and wedges you can plan for less release but it's entirely dependent on course conditions too.

Not to mention the flag is **rarely the right shot**. Unless it's in the fat part of the green and you have a wedge in hand, aiming at the flag will usually lead to more bogeys (or doubles) than it will birdies.

Once you laser your distance and consider the other factors above, pick a specific yardage to give your subconscious mind a number before the shot. That doesn't mean you will hit that exact number (in fact, that rarely happens), but it gives your mind a clear picture of what you want to achieve.

Think back to the mental game section, the mind wants to help you achieve your goals. But you need to give it clarity on where you want to hit and how far you want the ball to travel in the air.

Before I start my pre-shot routine, I'll repeat my exact carry yardage and target. Then I'll step in and let my subconscious do the rest. Forget about the flagstick and focus on the yardage you want the shot to carry.

85. Mash the Mud

It's frustrating when you hit a great drive only to find a chunk of mud on the side of your golf ball.

You can always clean your golf ball if you're playing a casual round or playing winter rules. But if you're in competition or a more serious round, you need to learn how to deal with mud.

Where the mud is on your golf ball will depend on how it will affect the shot. If mud is on the left side of the golf ball, it will go right in the air. Conversely, the ball will go left if mud is on the right side. You need to plan for this by adjusting your aim and playing the mud. The longer the shot, the more left or right the ball will go.

If mud is in front of the golf ball, it shouldn't make a huge impact as you can still make a clean strike. However, if mud is where the clubface will meet the ball at impact, it will likely result in a less than perfect strike. In this instance, it's a good idea to club up and choke up, so you don't have to make a full swing. Taking a three-quarter length swing will help you control the shot with a lower ball flight that should straighten it out slightly.

Finally, please make sure you always clean your golf ball after you mark it on the green. To make more putts and shoot lower scores, you need your ball to roll smoothly on the greens. These little changes can help shave strokes without much extra effort on your end.

86. Laser in on Lay Up Shots

One of the most difficult shots in all golf is laying up on a short par 4 or long par 5 for your third shot. Or, if you hit a terrible drive on a mid-length par 4 and can't go for the green in two. Sometimes laying up is necessary but it's easier said than done.

If you want to play wicked smart golf, you can't lose focus on the easy shots. With lay up shots, it's so easy not to pick a target, lazily go through your pre-shot routine, and hit a poor shot because you didn't go through your full routine.

But if you want to set yourself up for a good scoring opportunity, you need to have laser focus on layups. Here are three steps to avoid getting lazy and screwing up an easy shot.

- **Do your homework.** Before pulling a club from the bag, figure out what distance you want for your next shot. Is it 80 yards? A hundred yards? Try to lay up to a distance that feels comfortable for you and the pin location. Oftentimes mid-handicap golfers will take 3 wood because they think it will get them closest to the hole. But as I mentioned earlier, a 3 wood is the hardest club to hit from the deck and should rarely be used from the rough. Instead, use a utility iron, hybrid, or lofted fairway wood that is easy to hit and sets up your next shot.
- **Narrow your target.** Once you have the right club, you want to establish your target in the fairway for your layup. Specifically, think about the pin location and try to find an aiming point on the opposite side of the fairway to give you the best angle on the next shot. For example, if the pin is back left on the green, you want to lay up on the right side of the fairway to give you a straight shot at the pin. Then try to make your target as small as possible, so you focus with 100% intensity. Your target should never just be "the fairway" as it's not specific enough for your mind.

- **Go through your pre-shot routine.** Just like any shot, go through your full pre-shot routine. It's easy to get sloppy and forget about this with a layup shot, but this is when you need your routine most.

87. Whipping it in Windy Conditions

Playing golf in the wind is a nightmare for some players. But it doesn't have to be if you stick to these three rules:

Rule #1. Study the Wind

The first step to weathering the conditions is not to rush the shot and go through your full pre-shot routine. You want to analyze the wind by throwing grass in the air, watching competitors' shots, checking the flagstick, and looking at the tops of trees.

This will help you understand the wind direction and how much it will affect the total distance.

Rule #2. Choose the Right Club

Studying the wind is key to pulling the right club for your drive or approach shot.

Then it's deciding on the distance you want to hit, even if the club differs greatly from normal. For example, 15–20 mph can be two to three clubs' difference, so it might feel awkward.

The ball will go farther when you're downwind, but it will also have a lower ball flight. When your ball hits the green, it will have more forward spin than normal, so you need to plan accordingly.

Meanwhile, the ball will have a higher trajectory and lose distance when you're hitting into the wind. When your ball hits the green, it will hit and stop quicker than normal as it won't have as much forward spin.

Plus, you can have a crosswind, so it might take some extra time to locate your target and club of choice.

Rule #3. Stay Patient and Commit

Finally, the last part is to commit to the shot and trust the shot you imagined, even if you're taking two or three clubs more than normal because it's into the wind or aiming way right or left to ride the wind.

Pick your target and trust the shot.

Finally, stay patient. When the wind is whipping around, it's easy to get frustrated with how the ball reacts.

88. Simplify Your Shots

If you're like most golfers, chances are you try to work the ball both ways on the golf course. Some holes you try to hit a cut off the tee when the hole doglegs right. Or, if the pin is in the back left of the green, you try to hit a draw with your approach shot. It makes sense... right?

Wrong.

Most guys on the PGA Tour have one stock shot and play it 90% of the time, regardless of the hole location or if the fairway doglegs left or right. While they *can* hit all the shots on the driving range, they usually play one stock shot on the golf course (aside from maybe Tiger Woods). Dustin Johnson loves his cut shot, while Rory McIlroy loves his power draw.

You should do the same and only play one shot almost every single swing.

Unless you have a tree or some other obstacle in your way, try to play the same shot every single time (regardless of if the hole or pins calls for a specific type of shot). If the best players in the world struggle in competition to hit it both ways, you probably will too. Plus, when you try to work the golf ball both ways, you invite the dreaded double cross which can lead to some big misses.

On the range, develop your shot - whatever that might look like for you. When the pressure is on during the round, having a go-to shot will make it easier to pick your target and commit to the shot. Play your shot more often than not (even if the fairway or pin position calls for the opposite type of shot) to score your best.

89. Choke Up For Confidence and Control

If you need to hit a good shot after a few bad swings or things are spiraling out of control and you just made a big mistake, choke up and take an extra club.

Choking up on your grip is one of the best ways to almost immediately improve your ball striking and gain control. When you choke up, the club is slightly shorter and easier and less can go wrong. It's also easier to flight shots down under the wind when you make a three-quarter swing. Plus, taking more club usually gives you a better tempo as you know you have plenty of club to get to the green.

Not to mention, don't forget lesson #69 - most trouble is short of the green. So if you do hit it too well, you will miss long and usually have a better chance of getting it up and down for par.

Overall, choking up helps you hit it straighter, slightly lower, and almost always leads to better contact. In fact, if you watch the PGA Tour, you'll see they hit a ton of knockdown shots like this.

Do not feel like you always need to swing with 100% effort. Choking up on a club and swinging 80–90% is usually a better play, especially for the everyday golfer.

Choke up when you need some extra confidence and control.

90. Manage Your Misses

◆

You're going to hit a lot more misses than you do good shots in your career. As Ben Hogan said, *"This is a game of misses. The guy who misses the best is going to win."*

The sooner you can learn to manage your misses, the better you will become every time you tee it up. Here's an example… On an average round where I shoot even par, I bet I hit about eight to 10 shots (at most) perfectly. Typically, most are just considered good misses and there are probably eight to 10 bad shots that I must recover from.

You don't need to hit every shot perfectly to play well. You just need to learn your misses (by gaining self-awareness about your swing) and hit "good" misses.

For example, let's assume a flagstick is tucked in the back left portion of the green. On the left is a bunker, which is difficult up and down that could easily lead to a double bogey. Meanwhile, there is tons of room short and right of the green that will leave you with an easy up and down.

As I go through my analysis portion of my pre-shot routine, I note the "good miss," which in this example is short and right of the green. I also call out the bad miss, which is left and leaves a short-sided pitch and might be from the sand. I don't try to ignore it as I've found it can confuse your mind. Instead, call it out and then focus on what you want for the rest of the shot.

If you have more "good" misses than bad ones in a round, you'll score lower more consistently.

91. Start Laughing and Learning

◆

When you hit a "bad" shot during the round, you have a few choices; get mad and upset or laugh it off and learn from it. As I mentioned in the mental game section, mastering your emotions is key to performing your best on the golf course. While it won't happen overnight, the sooner you can learn to laugh and learn from every shot, the better golfer you will become.

After every "bad" shot you hit, ask yourself... *What can I learn from this?*

You can learn so much more about your game with this attitude and speed up success significantly. While your ego wants to get mad after every shot (trust me, I get it), this kind of behavior is limiting your potential. Because chances are, there is a lesson or two that you can learn *if you* have the right attitude to *learn from* it.

Maybe it was the wrong club, you didn't go through your pre-shot routine, you didn't commit to a target, you let doubt creep into your mind, or something else. Or, maybe it was just a bad swing which is part of playing golf!

Learning is part of golf, but if you're too upset to get the lessons, you will keep making the same mistakes. As Steve Jobs said, *"It's impossible to fail if you learn from your mistakes."*

92. Recap Your Round

◆

One of the best things you can do after your round is recapping your score.

No, I'm not talking about whining to your friends about how you couldn't buy a putt or the Golf Gods were against you. That isn't productive and goes against everything we've covered so far. Instead, I'm talking about diving into your rounds and learning from them.

A post-round recap, with formal stat tracking or not, is the easiest way to identify your weaknesses and improve each practice session. I started this in high school and still do it after every competitive round (and a lot of informal rounds too).

I vividly remember back in high school, during Ms. Momsen's history class, I would track my round from the previous day, logging fairways, greens, scrambling, putts, and notes into a three-ring journal. This helped me analyze certain shots, holes, and parts of my game that needed work, which allowed me to practice more efficiently and eventually drop 50 shots in my high school career.

Now tracking your stats has never been easier. While I don't write in a golf journal anymore, I use apps like Decades and other software to understand my performance in tournaments. It's one of the best things you can do for your game and is the definition of becoming a wicked smart golfer.

A post-round recap makes it easy to identify your weaknesses, recognize your strengths, and track your progress over time. Plus, it makes it very easy to learn where to spend your practice time in the future instead of aimlessly going to the driving range and hitting balls.

Once you have a solid understanding of your game, you can work on what held you back from scoring your best in the previous rounds. As Judy Rankin once said, *"I keep track of little mistakes. I also try to make notes of the times when I'm hitting the ball very well. You would be very surprised at some of the very basic things that I go back to twenty years later."*

It's always better to have more information and swing videos about your game to look back on than not enough. Make sure to check out the bonuses to learn more about my favorite statistic tracking tools at www.wickedsmartgolf.com/book

93. The Two Forms of Focus

Golf is an exhausting sport, both physically and mentally.

The game requires four-plus hours of chasing a little white ball around the course, all while fighting the demons in your head, navigating the course, battling the weather, playing against competitors, and everything else; therefore, you get home after a day on the course and are completely exhausted. While it might not require the physicality of football or basketball, golf requires tremendous mental energy.

Think about your focus to help you maintain high energy levels and not leave the course feeling like you just went to war. Many players think they must focus hard for every minute of the round. So many players think if they didn't focus from the moment they arrived at the course to the moment they left, they didn't try hard enough.

While this is a good intention, it's why you might feel so exhausted by the final hole. Don't get me wrong; you need to focus on every shot to play your best golf. Focus on every shot, not every second of the round. As you get to the tee box or ball for your approach, it's important to analyze and go through your pre-shot routine. But between shots, you need to give yourself a break.

You need two types of focus during a round of golf; *narrow and wide focus*.

Narrow focus refers to when you're walking up to your ball and assessing your shot. For me, this starts as I Velcro my glove. Securing my glove has become a subconscious signal to my brain that it's time to focus on the shot at hand. This is when I look at the distance, lie, wind, etc.

After creating a plan and going through my pre-shot routine, I give the shot my best effort and accept the result. Then I undo the Velcro of the glove and switch to *wide focus*.

Wide focus is when you quit thinking about golf or the next shot you face. Between shots, think about anything other than your current round. Try to think about non-golf things like friends, family, gym routine, etc.

Not thinking about golf isn't zoning out or lacking focus either—it's intentional to recharge, so you're 100% ready for the next shot. You only have so much energy and focus, so you want to make the most of it, so you don't waste it all early in the round. This is necessary during a round of golf—otherwise, you will drain your battery if you're trying to focus for every minute of a four-plus-hour round.

Don't try to focus like a robot for the entire round; it won't make you play better. It will just wear you down sooner. Give it maximum effort on each shot by focusing when you need to and taking a mental break between shots.

94. Commit for Certainty

◆

One of my final course management tips to help you play wicked smart golf is to always commit to a specific shot. It doesn't even have to be the right shot, but you need to commit to give yourself the best chance of success.

Dave Pelz explained this beautifully in his book, *Short Game Bible*. He said, *"Every shot requires a different line of thinking. But as you make your shot and swing decisions, you must commit to them. You can't have any doubts when you're standing over the ball."*

There is nothing worse than standing over the ball second-guessing yourself. It rarely leads to a good outcome. If you're over the ball and still have no idea what you're doing, step off and restart your pre-shot routine.

Your first instinct is almost always right.

I would guess your instincts are right at least 90% of the time, in both golf and life.

As Fred Shoemaker said in *Extraordinary Golf*, *"Your instincts are extraordinary — but basically, you've gone against them from the time you first started golfing."*

While it's hard to explain instinct and intuition, I think it plays a vital role in playing your best golf. Your first instinct is usually the right line for selecting a club for a tee shot or approach shot or reading greens.

Trust it so you can swing or putt with 100% confidence and conviction. There's nothing worse than standing over your golf ball and not feeling certain about what you want to accomplish. Learn to trust your instincts and great shots will happen because indecision is the worst and something you control. Always commit to one shot to give it 100% effort to give yourself the best possible chance to execute.

Quiet your mind enough so you can hear your intuition and trust it often.

95. Accept the Result

Finally, no matter what happens, the last part of any shot is accepting it and moving on. Some shots will turn out exactly as you imagined; others will be considered a good miss. While some shots are just terrible and will leave you confused on how the shot even occurred. Like I've said often in the book, that's just golf.

Whether it's good or bad, acceptance is the key to moving on, finding it, and hitting it again. As Dustin Johnson said, *"Accepting that you will hit bad shots and becoming okay with that is crucial to help you play better golf."*

The sooner you realize that bad shots will happen no matter how good you get, the sooner you will become a wicked smart golfer.

Bonus Video

Don't forget to watch the bonus materials at www.wickedsmartgolf.com/book to recap the best ways to think like a wicked smart golfer on the course.

Section VI: Crushing Your Competition

Learn how to play your best when it matters most

I've always loved the challenge—it's just you and 14 clubs vs. the golf course, the weather and everyone else in the field. On tournament days, you're not only a golfer but a caddy, nutritionist, sports therapist all in one. Some days you have it all together and feel like the best player ever. Other days, you question why you ever spent the money to play and take time out of your busy life to compete.

The main reason I love tournament golf is that it's the truest test of your game. As Jackie Burke Jr. said in *It's Only a Game*, *"If you have never won or lost in a competition, you're just treading water. The only way to feel any real sense of accomplishment is to post a score. Even a poor score will fulfill you if you did your best."*

There's nowhere to hide and it showcases the brilliance of solo competition. It seems to bring out the best in some players and the worst in others. Plus, having a tournament to look forward to gives you motivation to stay committed to your practice routine and not slack off.

I've seen guys who claim to be single-digit handicaps shoot in the 90s, even if it's the same course they play all the time. Whether you're playing a $5 Nassau, a member-member at your local country club, or a USGA qualifier, the stakes are raised. You get to see how your game plays against other competitors and feel the pressure firsthand.

The best part of competitive golf is that you learn about your game, both your swing and mental game. As Michael Jordan said, *"For a competitive junkie like me, golf is a great solution because it smacks you in the face every time you think you have accomplished something."*

This is one of the main reasons I went to Q-School in 2019, to see just how good my game was under extreme pressure. While I knew my game was solid, I also knew it was far from PGA Tour-worthy. But I knew that going to such a high-stakes event would make it clear where I needed to improve. Plus, getting out of your comfort zone is never a bad thing in life or golf.

It was one of the greatest experiences of my entire life, even though I missed going to the next stage of Q-school by two shots. That week in Nebraska taught me more about myself and my game than any other event. When I returned, I had tons of new things to work on in my mental and physical games. Somehow, the experience made me love and appreciate golf even more than I thought possible.

Whether you want to qualify for the Korn Ferry Tour, become a club champion, beat your buddies for cash, or qualify for USGA events, this section will help you out. I saved competitive golf for last because each section builds on the previous one. Each pillar of the book has set you up to become a complete player, a wicked smart golfer.

Once you learn and apply everything that came before this part of the book, you're setting yourself up for success in competition.

Does it mean you will always play well in competition? Absolutely not, don't forget you're still playing golf. But when you master the mental game, hone your skills inside 125 yards, and think wicked smart, you'll have the best chances to succeed.

To make the most out of your game in competition, follow these final tips to play better under pressure.

96. Practice Like You Play

To perform well in competition, you need to practice and play casual rounds the right way.

Here's what I mean... I know guys who play golf all the time, but they don't play as they would in a competition, meaning they drag some three-footers, foot wedge from under some trees back into the fairway, and take illegal drops from hazards. That's fine if you're out for a fun round with your golf buddies.

But if you have a tournament coming up, you need to play as if it were a competitive golf event to get accustomed to the environment. That means playing by the rules from the first tee to the final putt on the 18th green.

Otherwise, you will feel very much out of your element during the tournament and three-footers become very scary. Plus, this will make it easier to identify your weaknesses and figure out what to work on leading up to the event.

Competitive Practice

While playing golf as you would in a tournament is key, you can alter your practice sessions too; this is known as competitive practice. This is very different from block, skills, or random practice like we discussed in section one.

Competitive practice is all about changing up the environment and getting you out of your comfort zone. This is key to playing better in tournaments and priming your game to shine in the big moments. As Dr. Sian Belock said, *"Understanding how your body is going to feel under pressure, and learning to handle it, is a skill. So putting yourself under even a little bit of stress when you practice can matter a lot."*

Here are a few ways to do it:

- **Putting**: On the practice green, use one ball and hit each putt with your full pre-shot putting routine. Make sure you go through your entire green reading process, pick your apex or spot, and commit to your target. Do this for nine or 18 holes to keep testing yourself and putting yourself into tournament-like scenarios. You can also set a number, let's say 10 putts from four feet, and by number 10, your heart rate will likely increase and replicate a tournament.
- **Up and down**: The second way to add competitive practice is to play the up and down game. On a green where you can chip and putt, go through your full routine and try to get the shot up and down in two strokes. Act like something is on the line - your first top 10, winning the club championship, or some other golf goal - to raise the stakes and put yourself in a competitive environment.
- **On course practice**: It's challenging to mimic a tournament environment on the driving range since we don't play on the practice facility. Instead, try to get on the golf course for some on-course practice. Similar to the up and down game, put yourself in scenarios on the back nine as if you were in a tournament. Imagine playing the last three holes or the last hole at par or put yourself in a tough spot on 18 and try to get a par. Go through your full pre-shot routine, pick your targets, and hole out every putt.

The more you can get uncomfortable in practice, the better you will get in tournaments. Use your imagination to make each practice better so you're ready for almost any scenario in competition.

97. Avoid Technical Swing Changes Before Tournaments

◆

There is a time and place to change, evolve, and upgrade your swing. Unfortunately, leading up to a tournament is NOT that time—in fact, it's the absolute worst time to make swing changes.

For at least a week before your event, do not try to learn any new swing tips or make any last-minute adjustments. Don't pick up any golf magazines or watch any technical, swing-related videos on YouTube. This is not the time to try and "cram" in some last minute swing changes like you did with a test in school.

First off, not much will change in that amount of time. It's like waiting to exercise until the day before your vacation and spending a few hours in the gym hoping for immediate results. Changing your golf swing or body doesn't work like that.

Second, it's easy to get too technical on the driving range leading up to the event, which can translate to extra noise in your head during the tournament. A busy, chatty mind never leads to good golf and makes it nearly impossible to swing unconsciously and get in the zone. This can lead to playing your "golf swing" instead of just going out there and playing golf, which is a good way to play fearful, timid, and uncommitted.

However, this doesn't mean you should skip practice leading up to the competition. Instead, when you practice, prepare for the event strategically.

Here's how:

- **Practice your pre-shot routine relentlessly.** See how consistent you can make it and time yourself on the range to see how dialed in you can get your routine. Don't forget, a pre-shot routine can help you

stay focused, fend off nervous energy, and give each shot your best effort in competition.
- **Practice your short game, preferably at the competition site.** Short game is everything when it comes to playing your best golf, especially in tournaments. It's usually the person who chips and putts the best that wins. Get to know the speed of the greens on the putting green and work on basic chip shots to evaluate how the ball reacts to the greens. Hit bunker shots to test out the type of sand and get yourself more comfortable for the upcoming event.
- **Play the tournament course.** Often, tournaments feel even more intimidating if you don't play the course frequently. Fear of the unknown can make it hard to commit to certain shots and feel confident on the greens. When you're on the course, hit shots that you might face during the event and ones you don't feel comfortable with. For example, if there is a long par 3 over water, hit a few shots in practice rounds to test out different clubs and shot shapes to rid yourself of anxiety.
- **Play on the driving range.** If you can't make it to the course or they only allow one practice round, practice strategically on the driving range. Try to play nine or all 18 holes on the range by visualizing your shots, picking targets, and using clubs that you will use on the course.

Avoid swing changes, practice strategically, and rest up before events to get the best performance out of your game.

98. Tee It Up with Better Players

The best way to get better at anything is to surround yourself with people who are already doing what you want to do at a high level.

If you want to run longer and faster, join a running club. If you want to have a more positive attitude, hang out with positive people and ditch those who whine or complain. Or, if you want to shoot lower scores in golf, tee it up with better golfers. As John C. Maxwell said, *"The better you are at surrounding yourself with people of high potential, the greater your chance for success."*

You are a product of the people you surround yourself with.

With golf, this means facing your fears and playing with better players, even if it causes some anxiety and you feel like you don't belong. Don't get me wrong; it's uncomfortable at times and humbling to play with more skilled golfers, but it's how you can take your game to the next level. It's nearly impossible to elevate your game if you're constantly surrounded by people who aren't trying to improve. Even though they don't mean to, they are holding you back from reaching your true potential as a golfer.

For example, I still do this by competing in mini-tour golf tournaments that allow some of the field to enter as amateurs. I constantly go out there and get my ass beat by guys who play golf for a living, but I love it because I know that it makes me better and I love playing the toughest courses with the most difficult pin positions. I've also played with golfers who I knew were better and bet money knowing that unless I played my best golf, I would probably lose money. Sometimes I won, sometimes I broke even, and other times I lost big — but it always made me get better.

When you play with better golfers, you learn how they think and get around the golf course. Plus, you can see if they hit it further, straighter, play more conservatively, and see their short game first hand. If you're a competitive junkie, this will fuel you to practice differently, improve your weaknesses, and figure out how to get better fast. Join a men's league, find a weekly skins game, and search on Facebook for golf groups in your area. The sooner you do, the sooner you will tap into new levels of your own potential on the golf course.

Regardless of who you play with, make sure to always play your game. Don't try to hit the same clubs, shots, or swing like the people you're playing with. Play your game, you are enough!

99. Perfect Your Practice Rounds

Practice rounds are like a comfort blanket for golfers.

What's great is that you don't have the emotions of a tournament so you can make a strategic game plan for each hole and have found them to be incredibly helpful in showing up prepared. This is not the time to grind over every putt and play each shot like a tournament or you can wear yourself down before an event. Instead, focus on these items below, not your score, when playing practice rounds.

- **Carry distances.** Use your GPS or rangefinder to measure the carry distance over bunkers, water, and other obstacles on tee boxes and approach shots.
- **Firmness and size of greens.** Watch how much the ball releases on approach shots to learn the firmness of the greens. Then, make sure to notate the size of the greens and where the ideal landing spots are on each green.
- **Greenside spin.** Watch how much spin you get around the greens so you can understand where you need to land chips/pitches to get close to the pin in competition.
- **Bunker shots.** Sand changes course to course, so hit some shots from the fairway and greenside bunkers so I can figure out the sand. This way you don't have to try to figure it out in competition and have a better understanding of the firmness.
- **Calculate slope for approach shots.** To get your distances dialed in, make sure to use the slope on your rangefinder to notate how much uphill or downhill each green is (since you can't use slope in events).
- **Putting**: Lastly, hit a lot of extra putts on the greens. Throw a ball marker or divot tool down to simulate pins in different positions that you might expect during the event.

Also, make sure you buy a yardage book and take notes throughout the round—especially notate the slope of fairways and uphill/downhill shots to each green. Then factor in slope during the event to make sure you have the right yardage for each shot.

Try to time your practice rounds accordingly; you want to play your practice rounds pretty close to the event to simulate tournament conditions. For one-day events, I like to play the practice round the day before if possible. This will help groove my swing and see the course is in pretty similar shape to the big day.

For multi-day events, I like to schedule my practice rounds two days before the tournament begins. That way I can see the course in similar shape and still give myself one day in between to strategize, rest, and get my mindset dialed.

100. Always Arrive Early

As you enter the world of competitive golf, please adjust your pre-round routine. When you have a competitive round of golf, the last thing you want to do is rush before teeing off. Being flustered before the round can set the wrong tone for the day and lead to a poor warm-up and rocky start to the round. Sometimes, it's just too much to recover from and might lead to missing the cut or not posting the type of scores you know you're capable of shooting.

Make sure to get there plenty early to check-in and go through your pre-round routine. You will need to check in, get your cart, pay for skins, etc. so plan accordingly. Don't forget to think about traffic and time of day to avoid any stress prior to teeing off too.

I do my best to get there at least 60 minutes before tee time when playing in competitive events if I had the chance to play a practice round. If I don't get a practice round, I get there earlier to check out the course, spend more time putting, and extra time at the short game area. Usually, green speed is one of the biggest factors to playing well at different courses so getting there earlier on the first day is well worth it.

Make sure to refer to #63 to revisit my proven pre-tournament warm-up routine. This will help you build confidence and keep nerves at bay before an event.

101. Reset Your Expectations

Throughout the book, I've given you a lot of PGA Tour examples thanks to their endless ShotLink data, which tracks just about everything. Hopefully, it's shown you that even the best players in the world don't always hit it 300 yards, attack every pin, or make every putt.

But if you're still under the illusion that the best players hit perfect shots, here are more stats to help you reset your expectations.

→ **Wicked Smart Fact**

Check out these PGA Tour Statistics from the 2021 season:

- **Average driving distance: 296 yards** (on the firmest, fastest fairways, usually with good weather)
- **Driving accuracy: 60.69%** (yes, the best players in the world hit only a little more than half of all fairways).
- **Greens in regulation: 65.14%**
- **Scrambling: 57.94%**
- **Putting: 29.01 putts per round**

Hopefully, these statistics give you some perspective on what you should expect from your game, especially in tournaments. Don't expect to hit 14/14 fairways and 18/18 greens because even the pros don't get close to perfection. Instead, play with what you have that day, stay present, and don't force any shots just because it's a tournament.

Remember to give yourself a break, play *your* game, and I bet you'll play better in competition.

102. Patience and Persistence Are Key

◆

When you play in competitive events, it's easy to want to come out bombing drives and firing at every flag. But the truth is you never know when the magic will strike. It might happen on the first few holes, the middle of the round, or even on the back nine.

The point is don't force it early if you're just not feeling the magic (yet). You can't win the event in the first few holes or even the front nine, but you can lose it by playing too aggressively.

A few weeks before I finished this book I learned this lesson again. I started the round off as bad as I could with a triple bogey and two double bogeys. It would've been easy to mentally give up and throw in the towel, but I stuck with it. Despite the awful start, I went on a heater with four birdies in a row in the middle of the round (including a chip in). Then had a few pars and finished with back to back birdies and had seven on the round!

Sometimes, you have to feel out your swing, the course, and the greens. Don't try to force it early or press too hard on difficult holes. Instead, have a plan for each hole heading into the event, adapt to the conditions, and play your game. As Gary Player said, *"A good golfer has the determination to win and the patience to wait for the breaks."*

When you do get a good break, pounce on it. And when you're playing well, stay focused and don't let your foot off the gas. Stay patient and trust your game, sometimes the magic won't happen until the end of the round.

103. Maintain a Mantra

◆

A pre-shot routine will help you in competitive golf more than you could imagine. But a pre-shot routine is only there for you as you walk up to the golf ball.

Sometimes adopting a short mantra you can repeat to yourself between shots is a good idea too. It helps keep your nerves at bay and anxiety down between shots. As Gurudev Sri Sri Ravi Shankar said, *"Mantras bring out all the positive energy inside you. A mantra creates the sense of an armor around your body."*

I like to keep my mantras short and simple so they're easy to repeat. You want to choose each word intentionally to create the most powerful mantra.

Some mantras I've used include:

- *"I got this."*
- *"I am excited to be here."*
- *"I am the greatest."* (This one worked well for Muhammad Ali too.)

When creating your own golf mantra, make sure to:

- **Keep it short**. Choose each word with intention, so it's only a short sentence that is easy to remember and repeat.
- **Only use positive words**. As I've stressed in this book, it's so important to focus on what you want, not what you don't want. Make sure your mantra only uses positive, inspiring words.
- **Say it with energy**. Each time you repeat the mantra, say with it some vigor and strength. Reinforce the mantra with your body so you can make it happen.

104. Master Match Play

◆

Match play is so much fun and one of the reasons golf is such a legendary game. It's a new game within the game as scoring is 100% different. In match play, it's you vs. one other person, not the rest of the field. If you lose by four shots on the hole, you're only one down.

Match play is one reason why the Ryder Cup is so much fun to watch—it's different and requires a different type of strategy. Try to find events where you can compete in match play vs. traditional stroke play. It's a nice change-up from normal rounds of golf and brings a new element to the game.

When you play a match play event, you need to change your mindset drastically. You're no longer trying to beat the course; you only must beat your opponent. You must learn to quit worrying about setting course records and instead focus on beating your opponent above all else.

Here are my biggest tips to match play:

- **Give them short putts early**. Then, later in the round, make them putt a few short ones. Since they haven't had to make many clutch short putts yet, it'll make them pay a little extra attention and they might slip up.
- **Lay back off the tee**. I got this tip from Tiger Woods and think it's genius. Sometimes it's a good idea to lay back off the tee so you can have the first approach shot to the green. This way, you can put the pressure on them and hopefully stick one close.
- **Stay aggressive**. When things are going your way and your swing is on fire, keep playing aggressively.

Finally, the last tip for match play is to assume your competitor will always pull off the impossible. Plan for them to make long putts, chip in, and have other favorable breaks. I can't explain the logic but I've seen some crazy stuff happen in match play that doesn't seem to happen in stroke play events. Keep grinding until the hole is over and never let your foot off the gas until you get the W for the hole.

105. Anticipate Adrenaline

One of the reasons I think all golfers should play in tournaments is to feel the adrenaline rush. It's unreal how much of a jolt to your system it is and how great it feels to test your game in competition. I'll give you one warning: playing in tournaments is addicting and why I play in 50+ competitive days each year.

To play wicked smart in tournaments, you need to think about adrenaline as it plays a big role and not something you can easily simulate in practice. This is how you need to adjust for adrenaline on the golf course.

- **Full shots**: When hitting full shots, adrenaline adds more power to your game. If you are in between clubs, it's better to take the shorter club and trust the adrenaline. I've hit iron shots in tournaments that go 10 yards further and drives that go 20 yards longer than normal. While it's not going to happen every shot of every event, when you feel your blood pumping, play for adrenaline and trust your gut.
- **Putting**: While adrenaline will give you super strength to hit it longer than ever, it does the exact opposite with putting. That's why you see so many players leave putts short when they need to make a putt to win or tie on the 18th hole. Damn adrenaline! So when you find yourself with adrenaline, give yourself a little reminder to hit it slightly harder and get the ball to the hole. Remember, putts have zero percent chance of going in

Adrenaline is part of the game but you can learn to control it and adapt during the round. As Mac O'Grady said, *"You must attain a neurological and biological serenity in chaos. You cannot let yourself be sabotaged by adrenaline."*

These are general rules for adrenaline in golf but make sure to maintain self-awareness at the moment. Remember to use your breath, control your thoughts, and stick to your pre-shot routine to get the most from your game in tournaments.

106. Quit Worrying About Others

◆

As humans, most of us care too much about what others think of us. This happens in all aspects of life, including golf. It is human nature to care because our brains are literally hardwired to want others to like us. In the past, being liked by others meant staying a part of the tribe and not getting eaten by a Saber tooth tiger.

But we don't have to worry about wild animals for our survival anymore, yet that part of our brain hasn't evolved. So it makes it easy to worry about what other people think about our game, especially in competition.

I remember so many times in high school and college events when I was playing poorly and mid-round I would think, "What are people going to say about me?"

That's a terrible question to ask yourself and won't lead to playing better.

To play your best golf, you can't worry about the opinion of others.

Aaron Eckhart said it best, *"The day you stop caring what other people think of you is the day your life begins."*

Because here's the thing; no matter good or bad you play, someone will still always judge you. If you play well, there will be haters trying to bring you down and say it was a fluke. If you play badly, there will be people who judge you as well with an "I told you so" attitude. Let the Golf Gods handle their karma, it's not worth your time and mental space.

Golf is not like other sports where you get better every day, week, or month.

While it will happen in the beginning of your golfing career, the better you get, the harder it is to always see noticeable improvement. Sometimes you might have a bad week or even month but learn valuable lessons that help you take your game to the next level. It's all part of the process, even if it's frustrating at times.

Block out the noise and stop caring about the opinion of others to play your best.

107. Nail Your Nutrition

◆

To play your best golf in competition, you need enough energy to make it happen. While I'm far from a nutritionist, I know that keeping your energy levels high is key to staying mentally sharp in competition.

Every player is different as some love to have a big meal two hours before tee time, others fast, and others snack all day. Honestly, there isn't one way to do it, but it's always a good idea to have more food, snacks, and liquids than not enough. I don't want you getting Hulk angry on the golf course!

I'll leave the food choices up to you but will say hydration is important. According to Sponer, *"Dehydration can not only impact your performance physically but it can also negatively impact your mental game. Your cognitive performance is just as important as your physical performance. Dehydration can lead to slower reaction times, increased fatigue, and poor concentration."*

Your golf game depends on your hydration!

Here are three ways to improve your hydration in performance:

- Before the event, consume lots of water leading to it and several days prior.
- During the event, drink regularly and don't wait until your body tells you it's thirsty. If it's really hot, consider adding electrolytes or salts as well.
- After the event, make sure to keep hydrating, especially if you play in warm weather, and compete in multiple-day events. Refuel with water, sports drinks, electrolytes, and protein shakes.

Golf requires a ton of mental abilities and you need your mind as sharp as possible so that you can make the right decisions for each shot. Stay hydrated; your brain will thank you!

108. Exit Your Comfort Zone

While teeing it up with better players will help your skills and get your competitive juices flowing, sometimes it is not enough. Sometimes you need to do something that scares you to face your fears.

Here's an example.

Going to Q-School in 2019 scared the hell out of me. I was one of a handful of amateurs in the field and knew the odds were stacked against me making it to the next stage. Plus, I had to take a week off work, fly halfway across the country, and the entry fee was $3,000, plus my hotel and airfare.

Despite being so nervous I nearly passed out warming up, I made it out alive. Plus, I played some of my best golf, in the biggest event of my life. I conquered so many fears and became a more complete player in the process.

While it's one of my all-time favorite memories ever, it also made future events less scary. I went from competing at one of the highest levels of golf back to skins games and Arizona golf events. I felt at ease in normal events because I knew that my game could hold up under 10X more pressure. It's allowed me to keep things in perspective and helped with confidence in tournaments.

While I'm not saying you need to take a week off your life to do this, you can find big events near you. You can find mini-tournaments that allow amateurs or USGA qualifiers like the US Amateur, US Mid-Amateur, US Open, and more.

While the price for these tournaments is usually more than typical events, it's worth it. You get to play great golf courses with big stakes on the line. It's a great way to test your mental game against other great players.

109. Analyze Your Performance after the Round

One of the most important things you can do after a tournament round is track your stats and overall performance (lesson #92). But it's 10X more important to analyze all aspects of your game after competitive situations.

To do this, I highly suggest my all-time favorite statistic tracking program is Decades Golf. It's an incredible way to gain valuable insights into your game and learn more about course management than you ever thought possible. Plus, they now have the ability to track your mental game scorecard too.

While statistical tracking is great, I encourage you to take notes and record audio or video as soon as the event is over. You want to do this sooner rather than later as you're still in the zone and remember all the shots you just hit and what you were facing. I still go back to old notes and recordings to remember certain targets, swing thoughts, and my state of mind when I played well. Plus, as we discussed before, having statistics from every round makes it easier to spot trends and improve each practice session.

Although I encourage you to track statistics, some rounds are so bad that you just need to forget them. When those one off, poor performances way outside your normal scoring range happen, sometimes they're not worth it to track them. Occasionally you just have to forget them, take a few days off, and move on so they aren't etched in your memory.

To learn more about Decades and other journaling techniques, visit www.wickedsmartgolf.com/book now.

110. Continue Playing Competitive Events

To play better in competitive events, you need to play more tournaments. It's hard to play in one or two tournaments a year and expect to shine on the big stage.

Can it happen? Sure, but it generally comes down to getting familiar with playing in competitive events. The more tournaments you have under your belt, the less scary it feels and the more comfortable you are for each event. Soon, it will feel like a normal round of golf.

Increase your frequency of events to stay prepared and ready for the higher stakes. Plus, who doesn't want to play more golf?

While the first tee jitters will always exist, you won't feel as much out of your comfort zone as during your first events. Enjoy the process and challenge yourself to get into action more often to practice effectively and test your game under pressure.

111. Fight until the Finish

As I mentioned in the first section of this book, quitting is not an option. You must fight like the 300 Spartans at the Battle of Thermopylae until the very last shot of every single round you play - especially in tournaments.

Say it out loud: **QUITTING IS NOT AN OPTION.**

I can't tell you how many times I've seen guys quit after a bad front nine or leave late on the back nine in competitive events, all because they had too much pride to see a high score next to their name. But, again, this is just programming you for failure and giving yourself permission to quit in golf (and in life).

Never, ever give up in a tournament - mentally or physically. Take the high score like a man instead of walking away like a child. Plus, sometimes you have to figure it out on the golf course in competition, not alone on a driving range.

All it takes is a few good swings to get your game and confidence back. That could help the following day or in the weeks, even months to come. But you will never have that realization if you quit and head to your car.

As Jack Nicklaus said, *"Golf is the easiest game in the world to quit. But it's also the greatest game not to quit. Because when you conquer the game again, when you hit good shots again, golf is an even greater game than it was before."*

Keep grinding; you are only one swing away from figuring it out.

Bonus Video

Don't forget to watch the bonus materials at www.wickedsmartgolf.com/book to learn more about playing your best in tournaments.

Becoming a Wicked Smart Golfer

Hopefully, you enjoyed this book and have actionable steps you can take toward playing better, more consistent golf without swing changes. As you've learned, playing good golf is so much more than mastering your swing. It's how you think about each shot, your short game, and learning to navigate whatever test is given to you on the golf course on any given day.

The reason I wrote this book is so that more people can enjoy golf just a little bit more. Because let's get real, when you score better and more consistently, it makes the game more enjoyable. Don't get me wrong; I'm not saying your score is everything because it's not. But if you're always practicing and never improving (or actually getting worse), it's frustrating and might make you quit or lose your love for this great game.

Just remember, your swing is constantly evolving.

Your swing will change as long as you continue to pick up that set of golf clubs. But the good news is that a perfect swing doesn't exist, and even if it did, you don't need it to play great golf. Quit trying to master your golf swing and focus on playing golf.

To take it back full circle to our first lesson, remember that being able to play golf is a gift. Appreciate every time you're on the links and love all the moments that golf brings—the golf buddies that stay friends for life, the random people you meet, the business connections, the opportunities, and the endless memories. Not to mention all that it teaches you about yourself. Because at the end of the day, golf has so many parallels to life, it's almost hard to fathom.

But no matter how good you get, remember that we all have bad days and slumps; it's just the Golf Gods testing your commitment to the game. It's up to you to persevere, just keep swinging and never give up on the greatest game ever.

Keep using these tips and tricks to become a wicked smart golfer so you can shoot lower scores more consistently *without* changing your swing. With a consistent effort to play your best golf, I'm confident you can do more than you could ever imagine. I'll leave you with this epic quote:

"If you don't go out there and put in the work, you don't go out and put in the effort, one, you're not going to get the results, but two, and more importantly, you don't deserve it. You need to earn it. So that defined my upbringing. That defined my career."

- *Tiger Woods*

Finally, never forget that your best golf is yet to come if you put in the work. You got this!

Bonuses

Don't forget to check out all the free bonus content for even more tips to play better golf. Visit www.wickedsmartgolf.com/book to learn more.

Also, scan the code to easily listen to Wicked Smart Golf Podcast, subscribe on YouTube and follow on social media. I look forward to connecting with you and appreciate your support.